The Psalms Are Yours

Roland E. Murphy, O. Carm.

PAULIST PRESS

New York • Mahwah, N.J.

Book design by Nighthawk Design

Library of Congress Cataloging-in-Publication Data

Murphy, Roland Edmund, 1917–
The Psalms are yours / Roland E. Murphy.
p. cm.
Includes index.
ISBN 0-8091-3411-X (pbk.)
1. Bible. O.T. Psalms—Criticism, interpretation, etc.
2. Bible. O.T. Psalms—Commentaries. I. Title.
BS1430.2.M85 1993
223′.206—dc20 93-15639
CIP

Published by Paulist Press
997 Macarthur Boulevard
Mahwah, New Jersey 07430

Printed and bound in the
United States of America

Contents

Dedicated to all the Carmelites
with whom I have recited
the psalms over so many years

Abbreviations

ANET	J.B. Pritchard (ed.) *Ancient Near Eastern Texts* (Princeton, 1950; 3rd ed. with supplement, 1978)
lit.	literal(ly)
LXX	Greek Septuagint
ms(s)	manuscript(s)
MT	Massoretic Text
NAB	*New American Bible*
NEB	*New English Bible*
NJV	New Jewish Version—*Tanakh*
NRSV	*New Revised Standard Version*
passim	in several places

All references to the Psalms are to the Hebrew numbering of the verses. This may result in a one or two digit discrepancy from the common English translations. Because of technical printing reasons, the vocalization of Hebrew words is merely approximate.

Preface

The title of this book does not deny that the psalms belong to Israel in the first instance. They were written by and for that people of God, and were born of its beliefs and experiences. Nonetheless they are Israel's gift to you, whoever "you" may be. They are yours if you appropriate them into your way of thinking, in terms of prayer or aesthetics, or whatever reason may have prompted you to examine them. But before they become yours, you have to recognize how very much they remain also "theirs," the prayerful expressions of an ancient people in an ancient language and with a different world view.

We can be guided by the challenging words of two gifted German theologians. Martin Luther commented on Psalm 12 in the following words:

> None of you can pray a psalm if you have not previously made the words of the psalm your own. But they will then be your own when you have the same feeling and the same spirit in which the words were said. If you pray without this, you resemble those who play a role in a comedy, where the action takes place with proper words, but with a reality that is artificial. What a shipwrecked person really says sounds quite differently coming from the actor who plays the part of the shipwrecked, or a mask, even though the words remain the same. For the former speaks his own words, the latter speaks words that are foreign, and naturally with a different feeling. For the former, reality and words cohere; for the latter, reality is simulated.

In similar vein, a noted Jesuit theologian, the late Karl Rahner, commented about poetry and Christianity:

> Thus it is true that the ability and practice of perceiving the poetic word is a presupposition for hearing the word of God . . . the poetic word and the poetic ear are so much a part of a person that if this essential power were really lost to the heart, we could no longer hear the word of God in its human expression. In its inmost essence, the poetic is a prerequisite for Christianity.

With typical Rahnerian exaggeration, he touched on a profound truth that holds for readers of any or no faith. In order to understand the biblical word which is expressed in such highly poetic imagery, we have to be poets ourselves—we have to be able to react intelligently and sympathetically to the images and symbols that crowd the biblical pages. Unless we do this, we will not appreciate and fully comprehend the biblical message. Unless we exercise this inborn poetic talent, we will not make contact with the psalms on their own level. The purpose of this book is to give directions and guidance to those who wish to enter into the world of the psalms and so to make them their own.

In several articles and books (especially since *The Jerome Biblical Commentary* of 1968), the present writer has been occupied with the psalms. These writings were the fruit of many lectures and workshops for Protestants and Catholics, clergy and laity. The present work is probably the last treatment of the psalms I shall ever write. Experience has suggested two basic principles. First, one must read the psalms aggressively (not passively), before having recourse to a commentary or even to notes for help. It is this struggling with the text that enables one to appropriate a psalm. If one merely has recourse to a commentary to get the "answer" to a question, that is quickly forgotten, even though the explanation may have been accurate. There is no escape from initial reading (and rereading) of a psalm in and for itself. Not even the comment in the second half of this book should be consulted without the confrontation with the actual text of the psalm. Second, there are many preconceptions, many presuppositions, that we bring to the reading of the psalms (or to any book of the Bible). The first half of this book, a kind of introduction to the psalter, seeks to lay out these presuppositions in a manner that is clear and honest. First, there are various approaches to the psalms, or strategies for reading them: according to types, liturgical background, the attribution found in the superscriptions, or other methods that have been developed in the Jewish and Christian tradition. No matter what approach we personally favor, all these strategies should be noted. If we truly know the approach we are using, we can be aware of its shortcomings and be careful not to claim too much for it. Second, there is the world view that is present in the psalms. How did the ancients, over a period of some ten centuries, view reality: the world, the makeup of humans, human suffering, human sinfulness, and so forth? Often the world view is intimately associated with what we would call the theology of the psalms, but despite the overlap, the latter is worthy of special treatment. How did Israel view its Lord? What is the meaning of Zion, Temple, creation, messianism? This vast area cannot be adequately handled in a short compass, but it will suffice to point out key themes that need to be appreciated in understanding the psalms. Finally, some reflections on praying the psalms are offered.

This book is prompted by the appearance (1991) of the revised translation of the psalms in the New American Bible. The revision is the product of many members of the Catholic Biblical Association who submitted translations to a board of editors, who then revised these efforts in order to produce a translation that could be used in the liturgical lectionary of the

Roman rite. The board revised the translations in the light of the rhythms which liturgical use favors, as well as of the pastoral needs of a more inclusive language.

The history of the original *NAB* psalter is pertinent here. While it was translated from the traditional or received Hebrew text, it was guided by the approach to that text as manifested in the recent Latin translation of 1944, the *Liber Psalmorum*. The present revision has gone its own way but it remains a revised edition of the *NAB*. Occasionally a happy turn of phrase from the original version will strike a chord with the reader. However, the editorial board strove to reach a more accurate translation in the light of the advances in textual criticism, and thus the textual notes were also revised, and the explanatory footnotes were thoroughly redone by Richard Clifford, S.J. Equally important was another consideration: to render the psalms in more inclusive language. The goal was to preserve accuracy, but also to avoid unnecessary exclusive language in order to serve the needs of *all* the faithful. Hence a deliberate effort was made to avoid references to God as a male, since God is beyond sex, neither male nor female. The constraints of the English language made this very difficult at times, particularly when one is striving for a smooth translation. The principles underlying this effort to produce an inclusive language psalter have been published in *The Catholic Biblical Quarterly* 54 (1992) 724–26.

PART ONE

An Introduction to the Psalms

CHAPTER 1

Interpretive Approaches

a. Translations

Every translation of a work is also an interpretation. This labor of interpreting is inevitable because the receptor language can never quite catch the nuance of the original. Perhaps the Italian saying, "traduttore, traditore" (rendered freely: "translation is betrayal"), is an exaggeration, but anyone who has attempted to translate from another language appreciates its truth.

The fate of any literary composition, especially if it is ancient, is a perilous one in two respects. First, was it copied down correctly in the course of its transmission through the centuries? Second, if early on it was translated into many languages, as the Bible was, what is the quality of these translations? The ancient translations can be very valuable because they bear witness to the state of the (Hebrew) text from which they derive. The art of textual criticism—to approximate as closely as possible the original *reading* (not: meaning) of a text—is a most difficult task, even if it is unheralded. The textual notes that accompany the *NAB* translation are but a faint reflection of the arduous hours of decision-making involved in the work of establishing the text to be translated.

There was no special divine Providence at work in the preservation of the Hebrew (or the Old Testament) Bible. The complicated history of the transmission of the Hebrew Bible demonstrates the wide variations that are to be found within its books even before the Christian era. (One thinks of the long and short forms of the Books of Job and Jeremiah, or the complicated textual history of the Book of Joshua.) Traditionally Jews and Christians have fixed on what is called the Massoretic text (MT), namely, that form of the Hebrew Bible that was handed down in the Jewish community and rendered well nigh immutable by the notes and marks of the Jewish scholars or Massoretes during the seventh to the tenth century. The discovery of Hebrew Bible texts among the so-called Dead Sea Scrolls (discovered near the Dead Sea since 1947) proved that variation among texts existed before the Jewish community agreed on a received text that became the MT. This fact was not really surprising, because of differences in the translations of the Bible that had been made early on. The most famous is the old Greek version, called the Septuagint (LXX), which varied considerably in some books from the Hebrew. In many cases, this was not due to the whims of a translator (which must always be taken into consideration), but to the existence of diverse copies of the text. Only fragments of other Greek translations (Aquila, Symmachus and Theodotion) have been preserved. Origen's great Hexapla (= six columns), which laid out the Hebrew and the Greek translations in columns, was eventually lost to posterity. St. Jerome, the great Christian biblical scholar of antiquity, gave his life to the study of the Bible, and particularly to the translation of the Hebrew Bible into Latin, the language of the common people. This became known as the Vulgate, adopted by the Latin body of Christians through the Middle Ages (in contrast to the Greek form, used in Orthodox Christianity). Unfortunately, Hebrew was practically a dead language among Christians until the Renaissance period. But Jerome's work on the psalms is an interesting footnote to the point we wish to make about translations. There are no less than three translations of the psalter that are associated with Jerome. The "Roman" psalter was a reworking of the Old Latin translation (which itself had been a translation from the Greek version!) that Jerome made in the light of the Greek manuscripts that were available. The "Gallican" psalter is an improved edition of the "Roman," because Jerome was able to use the textual material that Origen had made available in the Hexapla. This came to be the accepted Latin translation of the psalms and found its place in the Vulgate Latin Bible. The third psalter, "according to the Hebrews," was done by Jerome on the basis of the Hebrew text. It was more exact than the previous Latin psalters, but it could not dislodge the Gallican psalter from the Vulgate, so popular had the latter become. These Latin psalters are more important for the history of the book and its interpretation, and its influence on the literature of the western world, than for text-critical purposes.

The complicated history of the transmission of the Hebrew text (a work that still goes on, vigorously, thanks to the discovery of the Dead Sea Scrolls) and the ancient versions is a warning to us to be aware of the differences that exist among modern translations, no matter how expert they are. Indeed, the general reader can profit from using more than one modern translation of the psalter.

Even more important than the *fact* of the disparity among ancient texts of the Bible is this implication: any translation is already an interpretation. The history of the interpretation of the Bible began with the transmission of the original, and the ensuing translations. The pertinent chapters in the *Cambridge History of the Bible, Vol 1: From the Beginnings to Jerome* (eds. P. Ackroyd and C. Evans; Cambridge University Press, 1970), provide an interesting presentation of all this background.

b. Literary Forms—Liturgical Settings

For decades biblical scholars have aimed at explaining the literal sense of the Bible, employing historical-critical methodology such as is used with any ancient literature. The goal was to ascertain the meaning the biblical author directly intended to convey by the written word. One of the means to this end is form criticism, or the study of the various literary forms used in the Bible. The psalter provides fertile field for such investigation, and the scholar who did the most to promote this methodology was Hermann Gunkel (1862–1932). He studied the literary types of the psalms, such as songs of praise, laments, etc., and attempted to situate them in their appropriate life setting. His approach was not without some precedent even in antiquity. The superscriptions to many psalms mention David, apparently as author, and a few even give specific settings in David's life to which the psalm refers, such as Psalm 3 when David fled from his son Absalom. This and similar attributions are creative interpretation, not historical attribution. We have no way of verifying the data which the ancient superscriptions supply. Indeed, the meanings of many terms, possibly musical designations, remain unknown to us (e.g. Ps 6:1, "upon the eighth"). However, the intention of the ancient pre-Christian notations was in the right direction; the ancients attempted to give a setting for the psalm. The designation of the setting remains a goal for modern scholarship, but most modern students have learned to be more modest and less specific about the setting or *Sitz im Leben*. Instead one speaks of a lament in the Temple, or a song of praise over a victory. There are many other mysterious terms in the psalter, perhaps the most famous being *Selah* (71 times in 39 psalms), the meaning of which is totally unknown. Another area of uncertainty is the music which probably accompanied several psalms. One need only recall Psalm

150 as a witness to the various instruments that were used with the psalms.

Hymn, or Song of Praise. Although in the Jewish tradition the entire psalter has received the name *tehillim,* or praises, the "hymn" designates a specific literary type of praise. Its basic structure is threefold: 1) a brief but joyous introduction that is a summons to praise the Lord; 2) an enumeration for the reasons to praise God; the two most prominent motifs are creation and deliverance in Israel's history, which are frequently introduced by terms like "for" or "because"; 3) a short conclusion, which may repeat the introduction (Pss 8, 103–104), or express a blessing (Ps 33). Some prefer to call these hymns "descriptive praise" (C. Westermann; see the discussion of thanksgiving below). Although there are slight differences of opinion among scholars, it is possible to maintain that the following are hymns: Psalms 8; 19:1–7; 29; 33; 46–48; 65; 66:1–12; 76; 84; 87; 93; 95–99; 100; 104–105; 111; 113–114; 117; 135–136; 145–150. This classification is based on structure and motifs. Examples can be also found outside the psalter (Song of Deborah in Judges 5; Song of Miriam in Exodus 15). Within these psalms certain groupings have been made on the basis of content. Songs of Zion (46; 47; 76; 84; 87; 122) have Jerusalem, the place where God's Name dwells (Deut 12:5,11), as their object. Others are called "enthronement hymns," because they celebrate the Lord's kingship: 47; 93; 97; 99. Perhaps 95; 96; 98; and 100 should be added to these. Sigmund Mowinckel (1884–1965) went so far as to postulate a feast of the enthronement of *yhwh,* associating these and many other psalms with this festal occasion (cf. *The Psalms in Israel's Worship* [Nashville: Abingdon, 1962]). Whether or not such a feast existed, the recognition of the Lord's kingship is clear. Some commentators propose that these hymns are to be situated in cultic reenactment of the Lord's enthronement, with a procession of the Ark (cf. Ps 47:6). In any case the student of the psalms should keep in mind that the Lord is hailed as king, and this rule is anchored in creation from of old and also in dominion over Israel, and indeed over the world which the Lord comes to "govern" (Pss 96:13; 98:9). The common exclamation hallelu-yah ("praise Yah!" i.e. the Lord; in Latin, alleluia) occurs in the title of several psalms (e.g. 146–150), and is itself an abbre-viated hymn.

Psalms of Thanksgiving. These are closely related to the song of praise, so much so that Claus Westermann would classify them as hymns, songs of narrative (or declarative) praise. He points out that properly speaking there is no word for "thank" or "thanksgiving" in Hebrew. The word that is translated as thanksgiving is the same word that means "praise," *todah*. The hymn proper seems to be spontaneous, and not turned toward self as the term "thanksgiving" suggests. Be that as it may, the structure and motifs of the so-called thanksgiving psalms are distinctive enough to deserve separate treatment. The thanks-giving psalm begins with a cry that resembles that of the open-ing of the hymn, "extol, praise," etc. The body of the poem consists in the psalmist's story of deliverance—how a cry for help was answered by the Lord, who is acknowledged as the rescuer. It may be that this prayer was accompanied in the Temple at a "todah" sacrifice. This seems to be the situation in Psalm 30:5–6 where the psalmist invites bystanders to join in the prayer and perhaps share in a sacred meal. There is a tendency to draw a lesson from the experience and to proclaim the Lord's faithfulness (Pss 30:6; 116:5–9; 118:6–9). In some cases there is a flashback, as the psalmist recalls the distress, and even the prayer that was uttered during that trying period (Pss 30:7–11; 114:10–15). There is nothing distinctive about the conclusion, which more or less ends on the note with which it begins—thanks or praise. However, the language of Psalm

30 is quite vivid: "you took off my sackcloth and clothed me with gladness" (v 12).

Among the thanksgiving psalms of an individual may be counted the following: 10:1–13; 30; 32; 34; 40:2–11; 41; 66:13–20; 92; 116; 118; 138. The collective psalms of thanksgiving (perhaps 67 and 124) are difficult to determine, since it is possible that the "I" in a thanksgiving psalm sometimes represents the community.

Laments. There are more laments of an individual (about 40) than any other type, and most of them are bunched together in the first half of the psalter: 3–7; 14 (= 53); 17; 22; 25–28; 31; 35; 36; 38–39; 40:12–16; 42–43; 51:54–57; 59; 61; 64; 69–71; 86; 88; 102; 130; 140–143. Among these may be counted certain subcategories, such as prayers of those who have been falsely accused and seek redress (e.g. 7, 35). There is a certain elasticity to the structure of the individual lament. It usually begins with a cry for help, or enters immediately into the complaint. The distress of the psalmist is portrayed with vigor and often with what seems to be wild exaggeration. We will examine the nature of this language later, but its presence should be noted. Often a psalm is so filled with imagery that the interpreter is hard put to state what the psalmist is suffering from (e.g. Pss 22, 69). These descriptions are softened by frequent invocations for help, affirmations of trust and loyalty to God. Often there is a vow to offer praise and sacrifice in return for deliverance from the distress. In many laments, but not all, there is an astonishing shift to a mood of certainty that one's prayer has been heard; see especially Psalms 3:8; 6:9–11; 22:23–32. There is no easy explanation for this change in mood. Is it due to the strength of the faith in the one who is praying? Or is the psalmist really praying after having been delivered? Many argue that since these are laments voiced in the Temple liturgy, one can presuppose that an oracle of salvation, or assurance, has been uttered by one of the

Temple personnel, and this calls for an appropriate liturgical response of praise and gratitude for deliverance. Although we have examples of divine oracles within the psalter (12:6; 35:3; 91:14–16; 121:3–5; cf. Lam 3:57), there is no real evidence of them within the lament itself. It is possible that a priest could have responded to the lament with words like "do not fear" (cf. Is 41:10,13; 43:1; 44:2), or "the Lord is your salvation" (cf. Ps 35:3). Such an oracle could have created the change in mood. Claus Westermann has characterized the psalter as a movement from lament to praise; these are the two poles within which the individual moves. However, there is little movement in such laments as 39 and 88. See C. Westermann, *Praise and Lament in the Psalms* (Atlanta: John Knox, 1981).

Communal Laments. In contrast to the lament of the individual is the action of the community. People would have gathered at the Temple on special days marked for fasting or mourning, especially in view of a drought or some other disaster (cf. the Books of Joel and Lamentations). Among these prayers may be counted the following: 44; 60; 74; 79; 80; 83; 85; 89; 90; 123. In general the communal lament is structured along the lines of the individual lament: plea for deliverance, description of distress, motifs for the Lord to intervene. These prayers are often prompted by defeat in battle (e.g. 44, 60, 74, 79).

The role of the lament among the psalms deserves greater appreciation than it usually receives. Complaints and outcries may be considered by some as not "prayerful." This is where the Bible has much to teach us. If we examine the structure of Israel's salvation experience, it is a movement from lament to praise, as the short summary in Deuteronomy 26:5–9 exemplifies: "A wandering Aramean was my father; and he went down into Egypt and sojourned there. . . . And the Egyptians treated us harshly. . . . Then we cried to the Lord the God of our fathers, and the Lord heard our voice, and saw our affliction . . . and the

Lord brought us out of Egypt" (Deut 26:5–9). The lament is an appeal to God's compassion. As Walter Brueggemann has put it, "Israel's history is shaped and interpreted as an experience of cry and rescue" (*Interpretation* 28 [1974] 18). C. Westermann (*Interpretation* 31 [1977] 263–75) has also noted this theological significance of the biblical lament. It speaks to the finiteness of humans and their needs. It is something of a paradox that the lament has almost disappeared from Christian prayer, despite the powerful words of Psalm 22 that are placed on the lips of Jesus (Mk 15:34). Anyone who would be repelled at the idea of complaint to God may be suspected of thinking that pagan stoicism has replaced biblical faith! Moreover, these psalms of lament are to be found throughout the Bible, most notably in the so-called "confessions" of Jeremiah (11:18–12:6; 15:10–21; 17:14–18; 18:18–23; 20:7–13; 20:14–18).

Psalms of Trust. The motif of trust appears frequently in the lament (e.g. Pss 4:3–9; 27:1–6), but it can also constitute a complete psalm, as in the case of Pss 16; 23; 62; 91; 121; 131. The motif of trust is the undergirding of practically all the laments: the Israelite would not, could not, have recourse to the Lord without it. The covenant love (Hebrew *hesed*) is the tie that binds them together.

Royal Psalms. This type is not characterized by a particular form, but rather by content: the subject is the king. Several literary genres appear. Psalm 18 is a royal psalm of thanksgiving. Psalm 20 (and 144:1–11) is a plea for the king's safety. Psalm 21 is a thanksgiving for the divine blessing accorded to the king. A royal wedding is the occasion for Psalm 45. It is difficult to be more precise about Psalms 2, 72, and 110 than to suggest that they are best understood as referring to the accession (or its anniversary) to the royal throne. To these may be added Psalm 101, in which a king lays down his style of rule (a kind of *miroir des rois*).

S. Mowinckel added a twist to the concept of royal psalms. He properly emphasized the role of the king as the vehicle of divine blessing upon the people. The king was viewed as a "holy" person in himself, authorized to offer sacrifice and intercede for the people—however unworthy he might personally be. Mowinckel claimed that many psalms were originally royal (e.g. Pss 28, 61, 63), but they came in the course of time to be "democratized" for use among the laity. More will be said about the royal psalms in the discussion of messianism.

Liturgies. In a broad sense this term would include practically the entire psalter, since so many psalms play a role in the Temple liturgy either by origin or by application. However, it is a useful term to designate certain psalms in which choral recitation is made explicit. The question and answer style of Psalms 15 and 24:3–6 is typical. They are not a kind of catechism; they seem to be entrance (or "gate") liturgies, a profession of faith upon entering the Temple to serve the Lord. Imitations of this genre appear in Isaiah 33:14–16 and Micah 6:6–8. It is worth noting that the qualifications for genuine worship are derived from the decalogue, and emphasize social virtues.

One can also detect solo voices and responses in other types of psalms, such as 91 and 121. An analysis of the structure will reveal the respective roles of Temple personnel and the faithful.

Finally some psalms can also be seen as liturgies of divine judgment: 50; 81; 95 and perhaps 78 (note the introduction in vv 1–11). The indictment of the people is given directly by the Lord (through one of the Temple personnel): "Hear!" (Pss 50:7; 81:8).

Historical Psalms. Various periods in Israel's history are reflected in many of the psalms, but certain ones deserve to be singled out because of the importance of Israel's history, and the various ways in which that theme is treated: 78; 105–106; 135–136. The classification is one of content, not form. Thus history is used for various purposes, e.g. to illustrate God's fidelity to the promises (105) or as a confession of sin (106).

Wisdom Psalms. This classification is a much debated point. There is no agreement on any list of these psalms. It is easier to speak of wisdom influence on certain psalms. The language characteristic of the sages has not been adequately studied, and it is doubtful if we have enough extant literature for such a work. Moreover, the language of the sages was also the language of the common people or it would not have been intelligible; it was not a jargon to itself. Hesitantly then one can propose the following: 32; 34; 37; 49; 111–112. Perhaps the most conspicuous example is Psalm 37. First, it is an acrostic poem (as is Psalm 34; each significant line or couplet begins with a successive letter of the Hebrew alphabet, a style apparently cultivated by the sages; see also the Book of Lamentations). Second, the various sections of Psalm 37 could easily be seen as fitting into the Book of Proverbs. Third, the opening lines take up a problem that figured prominently in wisdom thought: Why do the wicked prosper and the good suffer? (Of course, this is a broader problem in the entire Bible; cf. Jer 12:1–4.) If there are several "wisdom" characteristics, then one can at least speak of wisdom influence—whether or not there is such a thing as a literary wisdom genre (the best example of this might be the wisdom poems in Proverbs 1–9).

Psalms 1 and 119 are also considered by some to be wisdom psalms. However, the significance of the Torah (or "instruction") overrides the subject of wisdom. It is true that Sirach definitely identified Torah with wisdom, but no psalm can be dated with any certainty to his day (ca. 200).

Conclusion. The above discussion of the literary genres should not be regarded as written in stone. Over the years there have been various attempts to refine these types, but without upsetting the structure of the genres. The most interesting venture was W. Brueggemann's application of the psychological categories of Paul Ricoeur to the psalter. Laments were seen as prayers of disorientation; thanksgiving poems were understood to be prayers of reorientation, as one survived a crisis and was enabled to acknowledge God's intervention in personal life. The songs of praise were understood as songs of sheer orientation; they reflect serenity, well-being, the blessings of God. This grid does not really replace the analysis of literary genres, nor is it intended to. It does demonstrate the psychological dimensions and movements that can be detected in poems and cannot be frozen into words, however artful. Cf. W. Brueggemann, *The Message of the Psalms: A Theological Commentary* (Minneapolis: Augsburg, 1984).

We have not bothered to take up "mixed" types of psalms (e.g. half thanksgiving, half lament), but the enumeration of only certain verses in the lists given above may be taken as an indication of the existence of such types. More interesting, but also more hypothetical, is the problem of reinterpretation within a psalm, in which contrary voices are heard, balancing themselves out. This would call for detailed analysis and lengthy commentary. The basic facts are clear enough in the commentary below on Psalm 51, where vv 20–21 are in deliberate contrast with vv 17–19. In a way, it matters little that vv 20–21 may be a "later addition." The point is that they are present and add to the richness of the prayer by presenting a creative tension.

This first hermeneutical perspective has been a brief presentation of the literary forms of the various psalms that is widely accepted today. As we shall see, it is not the *only* vantage point from which to interpret the psalms. It has its weaknesses in that not all agree on the original setting of the psalms, and sometimes on the form itself (hymn? thanksgiving?) of a given poem. As with historical investigations, there is a certain amount of historical reconstruction behind the claims that are made. Some historical reconstruction in approaching an ancient literature is inevitable, and none of the perspectives which we are going to review in the following pages can escape this need. The question the readers will often be putting to themselves will concern the evidence for the reconstruction, the plausibility of the approach that is being employed.

Sometimes it is urged against the historical critical approach that it is exclusively centered on the past, on what the text *meant*. And even this goal it can only approximate. We are too conditioned by our own historicity to be able to recapture the past with exactitude; the very questions we put to the text are conditioned by our present situation. While there is truth in these objections, they cannot eliminate the insights into the Bible that this methodology has achieved. It is important to know all we can about the meaning an ancient text conveyed to its readers. We can resonate to the hopes and fears of the writers; the text does not become timeless and theoretical. Neither are we locked into the past. We can move with a certain continuity of meaning into the present. We do this with other literature (e.g. reading Shakespeare), and we can do it with the Bible. An insight into the historical meaning of a text will enable us to avoid faulty, even absurd interpretations. Yes, historical critical methodology is limited. But what it does, it does well.

c. The Psalms in Context, the Context of a Book

It is only recently that biblical scholarship has begun to emphasize the character of the psalter as a book in its own right, *one* book within the Bible. Hence a bibliography is offered here for those who wish to pursue the topic further. Not all of these scholars agree in details, but their general agreement is striking enough to catch the attention of all, and to add a new dimension to the understanding of the psalter. Brevard Childs, *Introduction to the Old Testament as Scripture* (Philadelphia: Fortress, 1979) 304–25; James L. Mays, "The David of the Psalms," *Interpretation* 40 (1986) 143–55; idem, "The Place of the Torah-Psalms in the Psalter," *Journal of Biblical Literature* 106 (1987) 1–12; J. Clinton McCann, "The Psalms as Instruction," *Interpretation* 46 (1992) 117–28; Gerald T. Sheppard, *Wisdom as a Hermeneutical Construct* (BZAW 151; Berlin: de Gruyter, 1980) 136–44; idem, *The Future of the Bible* (United Church of Canada Publishing House, 1990) 59–98; Gerald H. Wilson, *The Editing of the Hebrew Psalter* (SBLDS 76; Chico: Scholars Press, 1985); idem, "The Shape of the Book of Psalms," *Interpretation* 46 (1992) 129–42.

Two questions may be separated and kept in mind from the beginning. 1) The formation of the psalter as a book. Care must be taken to indicate the difficulties involved in reconstructing this history. A great deal of historical-critical methodology is involved in establishing any conclusions in this area. 2) Granted that the psalms were collected and finally combined into one book—is there a certain tell-tale evidence of the manner in which they are arranged that offers hints to interpretation? In other words, can one conclude to hermeneutical perspectives from the very layout of the work?

The Formation of the Psalter as a Book. No one will have failed to notice that the literary classification proceeded on the basis of form and content and that it treated each psalm separately. The new question is this: The psalms have been assembled in a book; they have been given a unity that separates them from other books of the Bible. What configuration has been given to them? If we even advert to the fact that the psalms constitute a book, we tend to dismiss this aspect and move on to the individual poem. Some have impressed us more than others because we have encountered them so often and returned to them as favorites. There is perhaps an analogue to certain biblical passages that we may have singled out, say, from Genesis or Isaiah. But in these cases we do not fail to be conscious of the context of the book or "author" from which the passage derives (even should it turn out to be, in the view of some, not "genuine").

The fact is that the psalter is a collection of poems—or, better, a collection of collections. The most obvious sign of this is the fivefold division which was created by the appearance of doxologies appearing at 41:13; 72:19; 89:52; 106:48. Within this framework, individual smaller collections can easily be pointed out, often by the data in the superscriptions. Thus, there are the songs of ascents in Psalms 120–134, the songs connected with Korah (42–49; 84–85; 87–88) and with Asaph (50; 73–83). The most prominent collection is the group attributed to David, about 73 in all: 3–9; 11–32; 34–41; 51–65; 68–70; 86; 101; 103; 108–110; 122; 124; 131; 133; 138–145. Even if the phrase "to/for David" in the superscriptions may have meant "concerning David" at an earlier time (a possibility), it certainly came to stand for "authorship," as the superscription to Psalm 18 indicates. In addition, the ending of Psalm 72:20 (even though the title associates this psalm with Solomon!) reads: "The end of the prayers (i.e. psalms) of David, son of Jesse."

There does not seem to be any significance in the numbers of psalms in each of the five "books": 41, 31, 17, 17, 44, but it is noteworthy that at least in each of the books there are psalms attributed to David. Naturally almost all of the Davidic psalms are poems of an individual; the majority of those attributed to the guilds of Korah and Asaph are collective in nature, and they are found especially in the so-called "Elohistic" psalter (Pss 42–83), i.e. a portion of the psalter in which the generic name for God, Elohim, is used conspicuously, and seems to have deliberately replaced the proper name, *yhwh,* in most instances (Elohim about 200 times and *yhwh* about 43 times).

Psalm 1 seems to have caught the special attention of nearly every student of the psalter. Whether or not it is classified as a wisdom or a "torah" (law, instruction) psalm, there is a particular quality about it. It is not a prayer; it is a blessing or beatitude which lays down the two ways of living, exemplified in the just and the wicked. The two ways are neatly characterized in Proverbs 1:10–15; 4:19; 15:9 and in 4:18; 12:28. In Psalm 1, righteousness consists in finding one's joy in the "law of the Lord" and in studying it day and night. The wicked will not survive, driven as they are like chaff before the wind. What we have here is an introduction to the rest of the psalter (which abounds in the righteous and sinners). Moreover, there is no superscription; the poem simply begins and with a few bold strokes and comparisons it summarizes an ideal follower of the Lord. An increasing number of scholars consider it as written to be a deliberate introduction to the book. Although it is torah, not the following psalms, that is the explicit subject (Ps 1:2), the rest of the psalms mediate the teaching of the Law, which is taken up again explicitly in Psalms 19:8–12 and 119. The psalter is being presented as instruction and not merely as prayer; this is really not a strange notion in view of the old saying, *lex orandi, lex credendi:* the law of prayer is the law of belief.

Psalm 1 is not alone in its importance for the structure of the book. It is followed by another psalm, also without a superscription, which gives one pause: Psalm 2. This is a royal psalm, dealing with the reigning king in Jerusalem, and the setting is difficult to define. Much depends upon whether the description of the revolt of the nations portrayed in the psalms is real rebellion or only a rhetorical flourish, part of the court style which was much more at home in the empires of the ancient Fertile Crescent than in the tiny kingdom of the Israelites. One cannot escape asking the question why such a psalm was preserved (and this would apply to the other royal psalms as well) because Israel ceased to be a kingdom with the destruction of Jerusalem in 587. The best answer is that the psalm came to be interpreted in a messianic, eschatological sense: in the end time, the messiah, a new David, would restore the kingdom of Israel. This was the type of messianism that was rife in the period just before and after the beginning of the Christian era, as is borne out by the fervent national hopes in the so-called Psalms of Solomon (60–40 B.C.) and reflected in the popular movements described in the New Testament itself. The promise to David in 2 Samuel 7 was eventually to be realized, and the kingdom of God re-established in and through Israel. When Christians pray and interpret this psalm, especially in the Christmas liturgy, they are looking back at what they consider its fulfillment; Jews are looking forward to its fulfillment.

Our main concern here is the relationship between Psalms 1 and 2, and their function within the psalter. At first they appear to deal with two such separate topics—torah and kingship—that no association seems possible. There is some evidence that at one time Psalm 2 was actually the first in the Book of Psalms. It is quoted (part of v 7) as "the first psalm" in certain ("Western") texts of Acts 13:33. In a few Hebrew manuscripts the enumeration of psalms begins with our Psalm 2, leaving our Psalm 1 unnumbered, although it is present. The point is not that these two poems were ever one psalm, but rather is there any significance in their (editorial) position at the beginning of the psalter? Scholars have gone on to point out that the first psalm begins with a "blessing" or macarism, and the second ends with one (Ps 1:1; Ps 2:11). Moreover, one can point to certain catchwords that suggest a relationship: the repetition of "meditate," *hagah*, occurring in 1:2 (*NAB*, "study") and in 2:1 (*NAB*, "grumble"); the importance of the "way" (1:1, 6; 2:11); the "counsel of the wicked" in 1:1 is in contrast to the admonition to the kings in 2:10 to "be wise and learn discipline" (*NAB*, "give heed, take warning"). One is reminded of the wisdom tag with which the

Book of Hosea ends: "Let the one who is wise understand. . . . Straight are the paths of the Lord, in them the just walk . . ." (14:10). Some have even urged that Psalms 1 and 2 give a certain unity to an introduction to the rest of the psalter. The perspective is not just the individual and morality (Ps 1), but the just order that royal power should preserve on earth (Ps 2). Thus, a double theme, individual and social, is highlighted from the beginning, and will be reflected in later psalms such as 72 (the king) and 119 (individual devotion to the torah).

Conclusion. More observations might be made about the formation of the psalter. But enough has been said already; we have moved from likely conclusions about the collections of the psalms into hermeneutical perspectives concerning the *meaning* given by them to the final shape of the psalter. We consider separately the cases of the first two psalms.

The first claim is that Psalm 1 is a deliberate indication of how the editor responsible for its positioning intended the psalms to be read. Brevard Childs has stated this well:

> The present editing of this original Torah psalm had provided the psalm with a new function as the introduction to the whole Psalter. . . . Certainly in its final stage of development, Ps 1 has assumed a highly significant function as a preface to the psalms which are to be read, studied, and meditated upon. The Torah of God which is the living word of God is mediated through its written form as sacred scripture. With the written word Israel is challenged to meditate day and night in seeking the will of God. Indeed, as a heading to the whole Psalter the blessing now includes the faithful meditation on the sacred writings which follow. The introduction points to these prayers as the medium through which Israel now responds to the divine word. Because Israel continues to hear God's word through the voice of the psalmist's response,

> these prayers now function as the divine word itself. The original cultic role of the psalms has been subsumed under a larger category of the canon (*Introduction*, p. 513).

This is a legitimate hermeneutical move; it is what has been called the "Scripturalization" (J. Kugel) of the psalms, when they were collected and made part of the authoritative Hebrew Bible. Or, to put it another way, the question of Dietrich Bonhoeffer receives an answer. He reflected on how psalms which were the words of humans addressed to God could be viewed as words of God addressed to humans—in other words, as part of God's biblical address to us. The position of Psalm 1 suggests how this is possible. It is a hermeneutical shift given at the very beginning of the book, recommending how the book can be read and understood.

This is as far as I would be prepared to go. I do think that Psalm 1 provides an insight into a level of understanding the rest of the psalter that is valid and valuable. But it is not the *only* way nor the only *authoritative* way of interpreting the psalms. It involves the same kind of hypothesizing from which historical critical methodology could not escape. Both approaches draw conclusions that stand or fall on the strength of the various reasons adduced for them. But they should not be seen in adversarial positions. They do not necessarily preclude one another. Both are *levels* of understanding with limited but reasonable credibility. This means that one is not more authoritative than the other. Indeed, the Bible does not lay down rules for authoritative interpretation. This is the work of the readers of the Bible, ecclesial or otherwise. And the success of such interpretations will depend on several factors other than mere authority, such as the context of the reader and the pertinence of various levels of understanding.

The question of the *union* of Psalms 1 and 2, and the hermeneutical perspectives which this opens up for the rest of the psalter, is a much more debatable topic. Two objections can be made against this position: 1) the basis for the association of the two psalms (indicated above, linguistic resonance, etc.) is not firm enough; 2) the themes of the two psalms are so very different: observance of the torah and subjection to the Davidic ("messianic") king. This double perspective weakens the advantage of recognizing the perspective which Psalm 1 gives to the psalter, and ultimately it limits the thrust of the psalter itself, which ranges far beyond the promise to David (2 Samuel 7).

We may close this consideration of the book of psalms and superscriptions with a consideration of the specific context which is sometimes provided by the superscription. It has already been noted that this occurs for 13 of the psalms attributed to David. It occurs also for other psalms. Thus, Psalm 30 is described as "a song for the dedication of the Temple." It makes no difference whether this refers to the second Temple (515 B.C.) or the feast of Hanukkah (165 B.C.). It violently uproots the psalm from the perfectly intelligible individual situation of its original composition and puts it into the realm of what has been called "corporate use," referring now to the deliverance of the people from Exile. One need not dispute the right of a community to reuse and reinterpret its own traditions. But such a superscription should not be used to dictate the more obvious and certainly undeniable meaning of Psalm 30 as a thanksgiving of an individual for deliverance. This is, by the way, the meaning that is established by historical-critical methodology, as can be deduced from the comment on it below.

d. The Psalms and David (The Composition of the Book)

One can hardly leave the discussion of superscriptions without commenting on the attribution of the psalms (at least 73) to David. What can be said about David is applicable to the authorship of the other psalms as well. The facts in the case are that we are simply unable to attribute with certainty *any* psalm to David. We cannot verify his authorship from any source outside the tradition found within the Book of Psalms. In some cases one can neither affirm Davidic authorship nor deny it, on the basis of content. There is simply no certainty. The tradition behind the ascription of authorship is not part of the Word of God. It is editorial (re)classification according to a venerable tradition. History has built such a case against Davidic authorship that its applicability seems doomed, and yet . . .

Can one make a profitable and hermeneutical case for interpreting the psalter from the point of view of Davidic authorship? It is obvious that the pre-critical period simply took the path of Davidic authorship. Is it possible for a modern sophisticated student of the Bible to do the same and to profit from such a contextualization? B. Childs and other argue in the affirmative; cf. B. Childs, *Introduction to the Old Testament as Scripture* (Philadelphia: Fortress, 1979).

First of all, situating psalms in the life of a human being, rather than in the liturgy—deculticizing them, as it were—creates a wider hermeneutical context, at least for the Davidic psalms. Childs finds that "the move toward universalizing the psalm was achieved by relating it to the history of a David as a representative man" (*Introduction,* 552). In other words, David is Everyman. The full range of David's virtues and vices, hopes and despairs, gratitude and lament is revealed—the emotional life of a human being with which we can sympathize. We go through the same kind of experiences and thus can relate to the David psalm.

To this one may respond by asking if it is necessary to go through these gyrations to identify with the psalmist (whoever it may have been). Why conjure up a situation in the life of David in order to understand or pray a psalm? It simply seems so unnecessary. Ultimately we are reduced to Everyman or universal experience. Why start then with David? Indeed the specific situations in David's life to which some 13 psalms are attributed *limit* the application to the current situation. It becomes an "historical" note about an historical character with whom one or other reader may find it difficult to sympathize. The Davidic authorship is a limitation.

Another claim is made by Gerald Sheppard in *The Future of the Bible* (United Church of Canada Publishing House, 1990): "The presentation of David within the book and elsewhere in scripture provides the key sign of the book's coherence, as well as the context of its interpretation as a part of a larger scripture. We begin to realize that the prescriptural hymns can be heard scripturally only when they are heard in just this association with David" (p. 84). A particular angle in this approach should be noted; the key terms are: coherence, context, and prescriptural. Each of these deserves some comment and also a warning: Sheppard's views are more subtle than this brief discussion can portray. As for coherence, is it not obtained at too great a price? Its historical basis is, as Sheppard himself would admit, questionable. Then, is not the coherence artificial because of an attribution of authorship that in fact accounts for less than half of the psalter? As for context, the giant figure of David can provide a certain context, and in many cases a fruitful one, for the interpretation of the psalms. But, quite simply, it is not a necessary nor the only context. As for "pre-scriptural hymns," if I understand the phrase correctly, this refers to psalms that would have been written and utilized up until the time they were collected and edited in the present Book of Psalms. This also implies that the titles are part of "scripture," and one should not depart from this view if one is going to give a "scriptural" interpretation of a given psalm. In other words, the psalms were "pre-scriptural" until they were provided with titles. This is to give too much power to the superscriptions. For example, G. Sheppard would admit that "the original psalm behind Psalm 3 had little to do with David . . ." but "it does now in the context of its role as scripture" (*The Future of the Bible,* p. 88). "We cannot make the Bible a better scripture by reconstructing earlier levels of its text and context" (*The Future of the Bible,* p. 88). One can agree heartily with the end of this statement about reconstruction of earlier levels of the text. But the implication that the superscription constitutes a text as "scripture" and also dictates the manner of interpretation is an exaggerated claim. The Davidic interpretation is just as much a reconstruction (on the part of the Jewish tradition—and its legitimacy is not to be denied), as the reconstruction of modern scholars (some of which may be valid—not all need to be defended). In other words, the superscriptions did not stamp the seal "scripture" on the final collection of the psalms. Rather, they reflect honorable and respectable tradition that provides *one* interpretive strategy in approaching the psalter. The excesses of some modern exponents of the historical critical method should not force us to reinterpret the superscriptions in order to maintain a psalm as "scriptural."

Another strong case for the validity of the Davidic interpretation of the psalter is made by Alan Cooper: "The Davidic attribution of the Psalms, in my view, is best understood as a productive interpretive strategy rather than as an historical claim" ("The Life and Times of King David According to the Book of Psalms," in *The Poet and the Historian* [ed. R.E. Friedmann; HSS 26; Chico: Scholars Press, 1983] p. 125). Cooper attempts a *via media* between accepting "a traditional positivistic mode of reading the psalms, rabbinic or Patristic" and simply denying "the veracity of the Bible's own claim about the Psalms" (p. 124). In this connection he quotes an important observation of Hayden White (*Tropics of Discourse,* 47): "To recognize that there is no such thing as a *single* correct view of any object under study but that there are *many* correct views, each requiring its own style of representation. This would allow us to entertain seriously those creative distortions offered by minds capable of looking at the past with the same seriousness as ourselves but with different affective and intellectual orientations" (p. 124). Cooper concludes that there are "only two sensible and productive ways of reading." One of these is the canonical shape advocated by Brevard Childs (discussed above). The other is "reading from an ahistorical aesthetic or literary-critical point of view." He explains that although the author is beyond our reach, "the imaginary world which is encoded in the text is not. . . . The meaning of the psalm is nothing more or less than the way we, as readers, appropriate the text and *make* it meaningful" (quotations from "The Life and Times . . ." pp. 130–31). Both of these approaches are possible. They do not necessarily exclude each other, and they will appear in the course of our treatment of the psalms.

e. Christian Approaches to the Psalms

There is no one monolithic "Christian" interpretation of the psalms, or of the Bible, for that matter. There are several Christian approaches to the psalms, and these can be exemplified from the New Testament, from the patristic and medieval periods, and from the modern era.

Without pretending to exhaust the variety and value of these approaches, we shall give examples that highlight the manner in which the Christian church has lived with and interpreted the psalms. In the New Testament the appropriation was along two main lines: the messianic interpretation of the royal psalms (2, 45, 72, etc.; see the treatment of messianism below), which had already begun in Jewish tradition, was now referred to Jesus Christ. Many psalms of lament were viewed as fulfilled in his suffering and death (e.g. Psalms 22, 69). It was in this fashion that the early Christians "explained"

Christ, whom they saw rooted in the biblical tradition to which they belonged.

The concept of the "fulfillment" of certain psalms in the life of Christ continued beyond the New Testament and is found in the early apologetic controversies, especially between Jews and Christians. Christian belief accepted Christ as the messiah, and biblical "proof," as it were, yielded little profit for a convinced Christian. A new twist was given to the Christian interpretation by the devotional life of the Church. As the psalms entered the liturgy and into the personal lives of the monks especially, the prophetic aspect was not lost, but it yielded to devotion. The interpretation remained Christocentric, to be sure, and perhaps can best be expressed in the *Enarrationes super psalmos* (a title given to Augustine's commentary by Erasmus). According to Augustine, it is Christ who speaks in the psalter, and also his Body, the Church. The psalms were freely interpreted on a Christian level, with little regard to the literal sense. This approach today is perhaps admired from a distance but hardly practiced. A recent study of J.L. Mays ("A Question of Identity: The Threefold Hermeneutic of Psalmody," *The Asbury Theological Journal* 46 [1991] 87–94) catches the spirit of St. Augustine when he describes the method as a reading of these psalms (he is referring to psalms in which the first person predominates) "as words that witness to the identification of Christ with our humanity" (p. 90). Here is an example from Augustine, commenting on Psalm 85:1: "God could not have given a greater gift to humans than to make the Word, through whom he established all things, their head, and to associate them with him as his members. The result is that he is son of God and son of man, one God with the Father, one man with men, so that when we speak to God in prayer we do not separate from him the Son, and when the body of the Son prays, it does not separate its head from itself since he is the one savior of his body—our Lord Jesus Christ, son of God, who both prays for us and prays in us and is prayed to by us. He prays for us, as our priest; he prays in us, as our head; he is prayed to by us, as our God. Let us recognize therefore our words in him and his words in us. . . . Therefore we pray to him, through him, we speak with him and he speaks with us" ("In Psalmum LXXXV," *Enarrationes in Psalmos* (CCSL 39; Turnhout: Brepols [1956] 1176–77; author's translation).

The Christocentric interpretation of the psalms was also furthered by the general typological approach to the Bible. This approach recognizes correspondences and analogies between various biblical figures or events, especially between the Testaments. But it was already to be found within the Old Testament itself. Thus, the Exodus deliverance became a type in Deutero-Isaiah, who described the deliverance from the Babylonian exile in terms of the Exodus experience. A new Exodus was to take place (Is 43:16–19; 51:9–11). Typology seems to be a mind-set of the ancient Israelite, and it is continued into the New Testament where Adam is viewed as a type of Christ (Rom 5:14), and the Passover lamb as a type of the Savior (Jn 19:36). And Christianity saw in David a type of Christ, the Son of David. The question that faces today's reader of the psalter is whether or not the typological approach is truly meaningful. This manner of interpretation continued well into the medieval and modern period. It was enshrined in the liturgy and in tradition. Early on, "Jerusalem" became the parade example of the various meanings that could be found in the Bible and especially in the psalms (the so-called songs of Zion, e.g., 46, 48). It could indicate the city in the literal sense. Its allegorical meaning (hardly distinguishable from the typological) is the Church and its doctrine. The moral meaning has to do with the Christian soul, i.e. the manner of truly Christian living. Finally, the tropological is the eschatological heavenly Jerusalem, the Church triumphant. This approach held the upper hand in Christian exegesis until the Reformation and Renaissance produced a greater sensitivity to history and the historical level of meaning of an ancient text. The historical critical approach to the Bible, although not without objection from many quarters, is still dominant. But it must be recognized as only one approach.

I do not think that reading the psalms from the point of view of their fulfillment in Christ is practical or fruitful for the modern Christian because such a person is already convinced of Christ's identity and role as the goal of Old Testament hope. Neither is the typological approach helpful. Its problem is twofold. First, it is somewhat discredited by the exaggerated use made of it by the early writers of the Church, where imagination often ran wild. Second, there is the perception that the typological approach does not appeal to the modern mind. Despite all the current emphasis on symbol, I think it is correct to say that the symbolic character of typology has not caught on. It seems foreign to our contemporaries, and perhaps the best example of this would be the relative neglect of the Epistle to the Hebrews. The indifference may be due to biblical illiteracy, but the line of correspondence between Old and New is not always clear or congenial. Other approaches are possible.

Rather than Christifying the psalms, we can read them as prayers originally directed to the God and Father of Jesus Christ, *yhwh* of the Old Testament, to whom Jesus himself prayed ("Our Father, who art in heaven . . ."). This God-centered approach remains close to the obvious literal meaning of the words and also to the New Testament ideal: "Through him [Christ], then, let us continually offer a sacrifice of praise to God, i.e., the fruit of lips that confess his name" (Heb 13:15). We worship God through Jesus Christ our mediator, as the venerable ending of the liturgical prayers reminds us: "Through Jesus Christ our Lord . . ." If we enter the psalms at this level we are worshiping the Father as Jesus himself did. It is one level of understanding and prayer—not the only one, but a basic one. We are free to go beyond it, without neglecting it. In a sense we cannot pray what we do not understand. That suggests that we should absorb the world view of the psalmist and go through the argument, the substance of the prayer, embracing its forthright stance before God. Is it possible that this approach could be also adopted by a non-Christian? In part, yes. The mediation of Christ would not be accepted, but the recognition of the God who is reached by these prayers is available to all who are willing to be nourished by Old Testament thought and faith. I would suggest that this view shares in the basic understanding that Jesus had while he was on earth. He and his followers nourished their spiritual lives with the directness, boldness and beauty of the language of the psalms in understanding the God they worshiped.

This may not be satisfactory for a Christian who wants to worship God from a more distinctive and explicit Christian viewpoint. Nothing can be legislated about this, since movement in prayer is a matter of following the lead of the Spirit. For example, a Christian need not restrict himself or herself to the Old Testament notion of life, Sheol, and death—to the exclusion of eternal life with God. Such a person reads many Old Testament texts with a fuller meaning, and this is quite legitimate. We can understand texts such as Psalm 16:11 in an eschatological sense:

> You will show me the path to life,
> abounding joy in your presence,
> the delights at your right hand forever.

At the same time we should heed Dietrich Bonhoeffer's words about "cheap grace," and not fail to appreciate the level of meaning that is intended by the psalmist. It was life in the here and now that is meant, not the next life—and this is surely an important component of religious aspirations. It is not uncommon to hear comments made with some amazement: "How did they believe in God?" (since they had no idea of a future life!). This kind of reaction shows how much Christians need to assimilate the Old Testament understanding of God and of life if they would appreciate what the New Testament offers them.

In his *Letters and Papers from Prison* (rev. ed.; E. Bethge trans.; New York: Macmillan, 1986) p. 86, Dietrich Bonhoeffer set down some words for all Christians to take to heart:

> My thoughts and feelings seem to be getting more and more like those of the Old Testament, and in recent months I have been reading the Old Testament much more than the New. It is only when one knows the unutterability of the name of God that one can utter the name of Jesus Christ; it is only when one loves life and the earth so much that without them everything seems to be over that one can believe in the resurrection and a new world. . . . In my opinion, it is not Christian to want to take our thoughts and feelings too quickly and too directly from the New Testament.

One may recognize in these words a certain exaggeration, but the exaggeration is in the right direction. The reverence that Israel and the Jews had for the sacred name, *yhwh,* was manifest in their substitution of another term for it (Adonai). This is not superstition; it comes from a profound sense of the divine, of who God is. The older Bible translations kept to this tradition: *Kyrios, Dominus,* LORD. Some moderns insist on Yahweh (the probable vocalization of the consonants of the tetragrammaton, *yhwh*), but this smacks of faddishness. The unutterability, the unsayability, of God's name, the divine transcendence, must be the basis for any faith in Christ—to utter the name of Christ who called *yhwh* "Father." Similarly with the doctrine of the resurrection which is so glibly accepted by many Christians; it is not appreciated, not even really understood, unless God's creation is first understood.

CHAPTER 2

Theological Considerations

a. Terminology: Some Key Words and Concepts

It is very important for the modern reader to be aware of the different categories of thought and understanding that underlie biblical expressions. In some cases it is practically impossible to separate world view from theology. Often the theological statements (e.g. about creation) are inextricably related to the world view of the ancient Israelite. We tend to project into the Bible our mentality, our own understanding of self and world. Thus we flatten out the biblical word, its imaginative quality, in favor of our own categories. We fail to savor the imagery and to enter into the world of thought in which Israel moved. To that extent we are impoverished, and even exposed to mistaking the biblical message.

We may take as an example the term "God," or "sons of God," or "gods." Monotheism is simply taken for granted by most readers of the Bible. Is not this one of the great triumphs of Israelite religion—that it bequeathed monotheism to the Western world? We accept monotheism, which is a tremendously creative idea, as a tidy little package that simply was a matter of saying the prayer of the *Shema:* "Hear, O Israel: The Lord is our God, the Lord alone" (Deut 6:4). Instant monotheism! No, this confession of the Lord's uniqueness is at the end of a long development. In the early days of Israel there was a comfortable polytheism that was shared with neighboring states and religions. There were in fact many gods, but it was seen that the Lord was unique among these, the first among equals. Hence we hear the exultant cry in many places: "Who is like to you among the gods?!" (Ex 15:11; Ps 77:16). Such statements are not monotheistic. They do not deny, rather they presuppose, the existence of other gods. They are henotheistic: there is only one unique Lord, who cannot be rivaled by any other.

Moreover, this God is not alone. The Lord is surrounded by heavenly beings (or "sons of God," Ps 29:1), the members of the heavenly court who do his will (even the Adversary, or Satan, is among them; Job 1:6), who are sent on missions (like Raphael in Tobit 12:12–18). Psalm 29 calls upon this array of heavenly beings to praise the Lord. The Lord is supreme. Only gradually did Israel arrive at a pure monotheism in which other gods are in fact zeroes. Thus the frequent polemic and ridicule that it heaped upon them, as in Psalm 135:15–18; Jeremiah 10:1–16; Wisdom 13:10–19. When one reads that the fool in his heart says there is no God (Pss 14:1=53:1), one must take into account the active mentality of the ancient person. This is not atheism, or a denial of the existence of God. It merely states that God is ineffective, inactive—a kind of practical atheism that is borne out by the immoral actions of the foolish (Ps 14:1).

Another word that is subject to misunderstanding is the term "soul," which occurs so frequently in English Bible translations. This is a misleading translation of the Hebrew term *nepesh* ("vital force"; cf. "soul" in Ps 104:1) and sometimes of *ruah* ("wind," "spirit," etc; cf. Ps 104:29). For us the word "soul" carries Greek nuances: the "spiritual" part of the human person who is composed of body and soul. These are simply *not* biblical categories, and we must avoid inflicting these categories upon the text. A human being is breathed-upon matter (Gen 2:7); when God retracts the breath of life (often termed "spirit," or *ruah*), living things die (cf. Ps 104:29; Eccl 12:7). It is only custom and the constraints of English language that lead to the use of the word "soul" in the Bible.

It is important for the modern reader to catch the flavor of certain biblical concepts, and to realize how Israel refused to raise questions or to philosophize about ideas that we take for granted. Thus, if the soul/body categories are not biblical, how are we to understand life and death? Life means that God breathes on all that live, thus sustaining them. At death the breath returned to God (Eccl 12:7); the body corrupted in the grave. Death means the grave, corruption, a shadowy existence (if it can even be considered such) in a place called Sheol (the nether world) that was usually localized in the belly of the earth. "Existence" in Sheol implies an afterlife. But the point is that there is no *real* life beyond death. Even though Samuel could be called up from Sheol (1 Sam 28:14), and David could speak of going to his dead son (2 Sam 12:13), the Israelites did not speculate concerning what went to Sheol. Perhaps this was because it was of no consequence. There was no *loving* contact with the Lord, only a whisper of existence about which nothing was really known.

Israel's resignation to the fact of death, its acceptance of Sheol, was not unique. It shared this view with most of its neighbors in the Fertile Crescent. Immortality belonged properly to the gods. The Epic of Gilgamesh is a story of a human effort to secure immortality, but it was ultimately unsuccessful: immortality belonged to the gods as Gilgamesh was told (*ANET,* 90). Hence there are repeated references to human life as something very tenuous; it is compared to "grass that dies" (Ps 90:5); the psalmist "withers like the grass" (Ps 102:12):

> Our days are like the grass;
>   like flowers of the field we blossom.
> The wind sweeps over us and we are gone;
>   our place knows us no more (Ps 103:16).

You have given my days a very short span;
  my life is as nothing before you.
  All mortals are but a breath.
Mere phantoms, we go our way;
  mere vapors, our restless pursuits;
  we heap up stores without knowing for whom (Ps 39:6–7).

It is no wonder that the psalmist could only have recourse to God:

And now, Lord, what future do I have?
  You are my only hope (Ps 39:8).

Thus the same fate awaited both the just and the unjust. But perhaps it can be said that the just suffered more grievously. They perceived that Sheol was even more than non-life. It was life without any *loving* contact with God. Very often (Pss 30:10; 88:11; 115:17; cf. Is 38:18) the psalmists refer to this feature: one can no longer praise God:

For who among the dead remembers you?
  who praises you in Sheol? (Ps 6:6).

The point is not that one somehow escapes God or evades the divine power; Psalm 139:8 and Amos 9:2 make that clear. But the relationship that the just had in this life with the Lord is finished. (It is only at the end of the Old Testament era that an undying relationship with God is perceived; cf. Wis 1:15; 5:5.)

Because Sheol means non-life, it comes to be used metaphorically to describe a distressful situation in this life: sickness, disaster, persecution, and so forth. When the psalmist exclaims (Ps 30:4): "You brought me up from Sheol," this means deliverance from some distress in the here and now; it has nothing to do with physical resuscitation, much less resurrection. But Sheol is a powerful image; the term "metaphor" does not do it justice. Death and Sheol, which are frequently parallel in Old Testament thought (e.g. Hos 13:14; Is 38:18), are conceived dynamically. They are powers that pursue a human being throughout life. And as we all know, they finally get their prey. Hence one can speak of the "power" (literally, "hand") of Sheol (Ps 89:49; cf. Hos 13:14), from which no mortal can escape. This concept of Death's power is the key to the meaning of many biblical texts. Thus in the Song of Songs 8:6 love and passion are compared to Death and Sheol. What is the point of the comparison? Strength. These are the two most powerful forces that humans have to deal with; no one can shake loose from their grip. Hence it is a tremendous compliment to true human love that it can be compared to Death and Sheol for strength.

The term "heart" is used in the psalms with some of the ambiguities it has in modern English. H.W. Wolff calls it "the most important word in the vocabulary of Old Testament anthropology" (*Anthropology of the Old Testament* [Philadelphia: Fortress, 1974] 40). It is used, in a double form, *leb* or *lebab,* 858 times, and almost always of human beings, although 28 times it is used of God (perhaps Hosea 11:8 is the most famous instance). Naturally the physical organ is meant, especially in descriptions of sickness (Ps 38:11, "my heart shudders"). Because it is an interior organ, it comes to stand for something hidden, inaccessible; only God knows the secrets of the heart (Ps 44:22). It is the Lord who can look at the heart and not be deceived by exterior signs, as in the case of the choice of David over his oldest brother, Eliab (1 Sam 16:7). The heart is also the seat of many activities, such as desire (Ps 21:3) and other emotions. Its principal activity is knowledge. In Deuteronomy 29:4 the eye is for seeing, and the ear for hearing and the heart for understanding. The psalmist prays,

Teach us to count our days aright,
that we may gain wisdom of heart (Ps 90:12).

The key to Solomon's wisdom is the "listening heart" for which he asks, and which God gives him (1 Kgs 3:9–12). Of course in biblical thought sheer mental activity is hardly ever separated from action. Hence "heart" is also an indication of the will and decision of a person. In Ezekiel we read, "I will give you a new heart and place a new spirit within you, taking from your bodies your stony hearts and giving you natural hearts" (36:26). Sensitivity to God's grace is indicated here by the natural heart.

As mentioned above, God, too, has a heart. It is the source of the divine plans (Ps 33:11, "wise designs"). In Genesis 6:6 God is grieved "to the heart" for having created human beings that have turned out to be so evil. Hence it can be said that God "repents" (*nḥm*) about something that has been done or planned (cf. Gen 6:6; Jer 18:8; Jon 3:10). Obviously this has nothing to do with repentance (over sin). The meaning is: to regret or to change one's mind. Here again one must be careful not to simply transpose Greek categories of thought (God is "pure act"; how can God "change"?) into a biblical framework. The Hebrew mind had no difficulty in God who *reacts,* even a God who suffers (e.g. Hos 11:1–9; 13:4–15).

Another part of the human body that is frequently mentioned are kidneys, which most English translations gloss with more "suitable" English words such as heart or mind or soul. Most often it is paired with "heart" and it designates the deepest feelings; cf. Pss 7:10; 16:7; 73:21). Even the word "liver" is used and is translated as "soul" in Psalm 16:9, or "heart" in Psalm 108:1, but it is often interpreted as "glory" or "honor" as in Psalm 7:6.

"Flesh" frequently connotes the sexual sphere in English.

But in the Bible it means simply the human, as opposed to the divine. We read in Isaiah:

> The Egyptians are human, and not God;
> their horses are flesh, and not spirit (Is 31:3).

What might at first look like a banal statement is a cutting comment about the vaunted Egyptian power; they belong to the human sphere. The psalmist trusts in God: "What can mere flesh do to me?" (Ps 54:6). In a more benign usage, God remembers that the people are flesh and withdraws the divine anger (Ps 78:23). The realm of the flesh is frailty, just as the realm of the spirit is strength and life (Job 34:14–15).

The word "name," one would think, should cause no one any trouble. We read in Genesis 2:19–20 that "whatever the man called every living creature, that was its name." We are also aware that individuals can receive meaningful names (*nomen est omen*), as the "Man," or Adam, is said to be made from *adamah* (ground), or Asher can be so called by his legal mother Leah because his birth has made her "happy" (Gen 30:13). The real problem is the name of the Lord—not merely in the sense of the sacred name *yhwh,* but in phrases like "in the name of the Lord."

God revealed self as *yhwh* (the vowels in *Yahweh* are an educated and probably a correct guess at the pronunciation) to Moses (Ex 3:13–15). In the course of time the reverence for the name was such that the term for "my lord" was substituted, and "Adonai" came to be said whenever the holy name appeared. The English translations have, by and large, translated the sacred name as LORD. All this is a sign of the tremendous importance which Israel attached to the sacred name. There is an impressive description of the Lord's encounter with Moses in Exodus 34:5–6, "The Lord descended in the cloud and stood with him there, and proclaimed the name, 'the Lord.' The

Lord passed before him, and proclaimed, 'The Lord, the Lord,' a God merciful and gracious, slow to anger, and abounding in steadfast love and faithfulness. . . ."

This feeling for a personal name is also to be found among human beings. In a sense, the name is the person. Hence a messenger is one who can speak "in the name of" the sender. And the name can also indicate the nature of a person (1 Sam 1:25, "Nabal [folly] is his name, and folly is with him"). A change of name pointed to the superiority and power of the one who made the change (Abram to Abraham, Gen 17:5). One can also appreciate the manner in which Israel wrestled with the problem of divine presence. The solution of Deuteronomic theology was that while the Lord dwelt in heaven, the *Name* was present in the Temple of the holy city. For better or worse, moderns have lost this sense of the power of the name. Hence there is scant comprehension of the significance of the Lord acting for the sake of the name (e.g. Ez 20:44, "And you shall know that I am the Lord, when I deal with you for my name's sake . . ."). Even the most significant biblical expressions have tended to become bland, such as "Blessed be the name of the Lord," or "in the name of the Lord."

Hence it is difficult for us to proclaim Psalm 8:2, 10 (a refrain) in a meaningful way: "How awesome is your name through all the earth!" Similarly, the spirited ending of Ps 7:18:

> I praise the justice of the Lord;
> I celebrate the name of the Lord Most High.

In Psalm 5:12 the Lord is asked to protect the faithful who are in need; the Lord is to be the joy and exultation of all "who love your name" (Ps 5:11). One can say that the name is shorthand for the person, but it fails to catch the flavor and fullness of the meaning.

The feeling for the presence of God is not unlike that for the name. There is no question that the true dwelling place of the Lord is above the waters in "heaven," where the heavenly court praises him (Ps 29). Indeed in one breath the psalmist proclaims a double presence, transcendent yet immanent:

> The Lord is in his holy temple;
> the Lord's throne is in heaven (Ps 11:4).

Israel had a deep sense of this mystery of the divine presence, as is shown by the prayer of Solomon in 1 Kings 8:27: nothing could really contain God, whether the heavens or the Temple. Yet the Lord was present to the people, as the liveliness of the language in the psalms makes clear. The psalmists were not talking to themselves; they did not speak "as if" the Lord was present.

Psalm 139 is remarkable testimony of this awareness of the divine presence. The intimacy is intense ("you have probed me, you know me"). God knows what the psalmist will say; around and about, the divine "hand" rests (vv 4–5), and there is sheer astonishment at such closeness. Anywhere in the universe, even in the heart of darkness, God holds fast the psalmist (vv 7–10):

> Where can I hide from your spirit?
> From your presence, where can I flee?

Of course it is not a question of trying to escape; there is simply an overpowering admiration of the divine presence. No matter what the poet can imagine—in view of the divine knowledge, guidance, pursuit, there is no escape (v 13, "even in my mother's womb").

Of course there was always the special presence of God in the Temple. Despite the mortal danger of seeing God's face (noted in Ex 33:30; Jgs 20:33), this is the phrase used to describe a meeting with the Lord in the Temple: "When can I go and see the face of God?" (Ps 42:3; cf also Pss 11:7; 17:15; 42:3;

and closely related, Pss 16:11; 27:4, 13). In a sense this was a spiritual or liturgical presence, for entrance into the Holy of Holies was not possible for the ordinary Israelite. No "face" was to be seen. In the Most Holy Place was the Ark of the Covenant, the footstool of the Lord, who was invisibly enthroned there, guarded by two Cherubim on either side. But the presence of God in the Bible is paradoxical. Sometimes the Lord is present precisely in absence—sometimes never more present than in those circumstances. The cry of the wounded psalmist is a direct appeal to God, even if the adversity that is suffered can be understood only as a rejection or at least a seeming rejection by God. The face of God is hidden (Pss 30:8; 104:29), or God is simply angry (Ps 6:2) or even asleep (Ps 44:24). Even in the most desperate psalm (Ps 88) there is the courage and faith to bring one's complaint to the Lord. Well did Samuel Terrien entitle his book on biblical theology as *The Elusive Presence* (New York: Harper & Row, 1978).

b. Creation

As indicated above, creation is one of the key themes in the hymns, and it figures prominently in many other books, such as Job 38–41, or Isaiah 40–66. Creation can be seen as a story of "beginnings" or as continuous creation that sustains all things in existence (cf. Ps 104). Perhaps the initial chapters of Genesis are best known and most often cited as the story of the beginnings. Michelangelo's frescoes in the Sistine Chapel render the scenes unforgettable; they are as majestic as the divine approval that creation was "good," and the unruffled sequence of six days is most reassuring. There is hardly a hint of a struggle in Genesis 1. The Lord simply commands. God has no trouble with "the formless void and darkness [that] covered the face of the deep" (*NRSV*). Elsewhere in the Bible there are clear allusions to what seems a battle with chaos, a *Chaoskampf,* in which the Lord seems to be the winner. The real battle is to be found in the creation stories of the ancient Near East: the Enuma Elish, in which Marduk disposes of Tiamat's cadaver to make the world (*ANET,* 67). The unruliness of the Sea is reflected in the Ugaritic myth where Baal engages in battle with Sea (*Yam; ANET,* 130–31), although this is not a creation story. The imagination of the biblical writers was a fertile one. As B. Batto has put it, they were mythmakers. They relied upon the creation and combat stories available in their culture in order to convey their understanding of reality; cf. B. Batto, *Slaying the Dragon: Mythmaking in the Biblical Tradition* (Louisville: Westminster/John Knox, 1992).

There is no logical description of the creative act. Many terms are used to portray the "opponent": the deep and the waters—personified in such figures as Leviathan in Psalm 74:14, the "fleeing serpent," the dragon that the Lord will kill in the sea (Is 27:1). He is merely a plaything according to Psalm 104:26 (cf. Job 41). Chaos is also personified as Rahab (cf. Is 51:9; Job 9:13; 26:12). As Psalm 89:10–11 puts it,

> You rule the raging Sea;
> you still its swelling waves.
> You crushed Rahab with a mortal blow;
> your strong arm scattered your foes.

Indeed, the conquest of creation comes to be associated with the victory which the Lord achieved over Israel's enemies at the Red Sea.

> Awake, awake, put on strength,
> O arm of the Lord!
> Awake, as in days of old,
> the generations of long ago!

Was it not you who cut Rahab in pieces,
who pierced the dragon?
Was it not you who dried up the Sea,
the waters of the great deep;
Who made the depths of the Sea a way
for the redeemed to cross over? (Is 51:9–10).

These images of chaos seem to have remained with Israel for centuries (cf. Ps 114; Hab 3:8–10). But Israel never seemed to doubt that the Lord's power over Rahab and Leviathan, over the forces of darkness and evil, would prevail. Some would claim that this is an open warfare in the pages of the Bible, and no victory is assured. Thus the persistence of evil and the problem of the suffering of the innocent might find an explanation in the intermittent "victories" of chaos. But the Lord is never portrayed as defeated; the conflict is apparently not one that he could conceivably lose. The texts are not alarming because chaos never seems to win out. As for the problem of suffering, the Old Testament does not give any "answer" to it. While conflict may be a human way of conceiving the problem and thus confronting the Lord with it, there appears to be an underlying belief in divine omnipotence (even if the word is not used). Otherwise, the use of the creation battle as a means of "moving" God to intervene in Israel's favor would be highly questionable. The myth was alive in the cult, where creation could be re-presented in a vivid way as conflict—but everyone knew who the winner was. In the wisdom literature there seems to be a downplaying of the conflict, as when chaos is portrayed as a babe in swaddling clothes:

Who shut within doors the Sea,
when it burst out of the womb;
When I made the clouds its garment
and thick darkness its swaddling bands?

When I set limits for it
  and fastened the bar of its door,
And said: Thus far shall you come but no farther
  and here shall your proud waves be stilled? (Job 38:8–11).

c. Salvation

Another important theme in the songs of praise is that of salvation. Very many different terms can be used for this idea: deliver, redeem, vindicate, etc. The hymns generally celebrate the "salvation" or saving intervention of God in Israel's history. Key traditions in the life of Israel will hover in the background as one studies and prays the psalms. They deal with the promises to the patriarchs, Abraham, Isaac and Jacob, which developed the initial word of God to Abraham in Genesis 12:1–3: Abraham was to become a people, receive a land, and somehow to be a blessing to the world. The Pentateuch and Joshua are the books that develop that story line—how Moses brought Abraham's descendants out of the slavery they suffered in Egypt to the land of promise where they established a foothold. Theologians have pointed out the so-called "little credo" in Deuteronomy 26:5–10. Even if it is misnamed, it is a neat summary of key events. To it must be added the Sinai theophany, the sealing of a covenant and stipulations whereby the mysterious *yhwh* became the God of Israel and Israel became the people of *yhwh:* "You shall be my people and I shall be your God." The tumultuous period of the Judges and of Saul, when Israel was threatened by the Philistines, gave way to the United Kingdom under David and Solomon. This period provided some of the key institutions and concepts in the psalms to which we must eventually turn our attention: Zion, the Temple, and royal messianism. The division into two kingdoms, North and South, or Israel and Judah, belongs especially to the period of the writing prophets. From them we learn of the vicissitudes in the history of Israel that led to the fall of Samaria in 721 and finally of Jerusalem in 587. It is impossible to measure the trauma that the people of God experienced (consider the grief expressed in the Book of Lamentations and Psalms 89, 137). The relatively short Babylonian exile of 587–539 was followed by domination under the Persians, the Ptolemies (of Egypt) and the Seleucids (of Antioch). We reach the end of the tumultuous period with the Maccabean revolt (168) and its aftermath.

The above paragraph summarizes briefly the kind of "salvation" which Israel experienced and related in the so-called historical psalms (78, 105, etc.) in which the sacred events of the past were rehearsed. But in most of the psalms, especially in the laments, the cry "save me," "deliver me," is not on a national level (although there are psalms of communal lament, such as Psalm 74). What is it that individual Israelites understood as "salvation," or "deliverance"? They meant safety from enemies, cure from sickness, shelter from unknown terrors, security from any impending misfortune. The other side of this was God's blessing, a restoration to health or wealth, and especially to the Lord's favor—to be able to visit God in the Temple, to share one's joy with fellow-believers, to be able to praise God once more without any sign of divine displeasure or wrath. Adversity and suffering were regularly taken to be a sign of sin, either one's personal sin, or the sin of the family or group. A calamity such as the destruction of the Temple calls forth the question:

Why, God, have you cast us off forever?
  Why does your anger burn against the sheep of your
  pasture? (Ps 74:1).

But they were also well aware of their own sinfulness:

> To you we owe our hymn of praise,
>   O God on Zion . . .
> To you all flesh must come
>   with its burden of wicked deeds.
> We are overcome by our sins,
>   only you can pardon them.
> Happy the chosen ones you bring
>   to dwell in your courts.
> May we be filled with the good things of your house,
>   the blessings of your holy temple (65:1–5).

There are many terms for sin in the Old Testament: miss the mark, rebel, transgress, etc. Perhaps the most expressive psalm on this score is the well-known *Miserere,* Psalm 51. As the late Bruce Vawter put it, "Three different words are used to express what the sinner begs God to do for him in his sinful state: 'blot out,' 'wash,' and 'cleanse.' All three verbs denote a ritual or declaratory obliteration of sin, but we must recall that the 'washing' the second verb alludes to is the washing of clothes—and the oriental flung his soiled clothing in a stream and stomped on it enthusiastically. So the psalmist is asking God for the two kinds of cleaning—what a later theology will distinguish into a forensic and a real justification. In the *forensic* justification, God simply declares the sinner to be a sinner no more. But since it is obvious that no human act can be done away with as though it had never occurred, there must also be a *real* justification. The guilt that has remained in the sinner and prevented his access to the God of holiness must be stamped out and obliterated, like the dirt in a soiled robe. The psalmist calls on the Lord to 'create a clean heart' and to 'renew an upright spirit' within him. . . . Create, he says, a new *me*. Sin was, in his eyes, an involvement from which man could not emerge without an alteration in his inmost being" ("The Scriptural Meaning of Sin," in *The Path of Wisdom* [Wilmington: Glazier, 1986] 54–59, at 58). The clean heart and steadfast spirit assured the psalmist of life. And life, it must be recalled, is life in the here and now, the good life: prosperity, prestige, a large family, the happiness and joy that comes from the blessing of God. There is only one thing that surpasses this life. It is the Lord's *hesed* or love, as we read in Psalm 63:4.

For your love is better than life;
  my lips offer you worship!

One cannot discuss sin without also considering its relationship to suffering and adversity. For the Old Testament person, the two were closely connected. If one does wrong, there will be punishment (in this life, of course). But if one is faithful to God, there will be prosperity and well-being. In other words, God rewards good and punishes evil. This general understanding prevails throughout the Bible. A typical example is Psalm 11:5–7:

The Lord tests the good and the bad,
  hates those who love violence.
And rains upon the wicked
  fiery coals and brimstone,
  a scorching wind is their allotted cup.
The Lord is just and loves just deeds;
  the upright shall see his face.

This law of retribution is accepted; God rewards and punishes. But could it be turned around? Was suffering and distress a sign of sin, of wrongdoing? And was the prosperity and well-being of anyone a sign of virtue? What about the fate of the innocent person who suffers? This gave rise to a quandary. It is the wicked, not the innocent, who should be afflicted! Many psalms question God's justice: why me? The argument between Job and the three friends (and ultimately with God) turns on the suffering of the innocent. The typical understanding of suffering and affliction is found also in the New Testament in the question the disciples address to Jesus. "Rabbi, who sinned, this man or his parents, that he was born blind?" (Jn 9:2). There had to be an explanation, if God was a just God. Psalm 37 tries to reassure the one who begins to doubt:

Do not be provoked by evildoers;
do not envy those who do wrong (Ps 37:1).

It was left to the authors of Job and Ecclesiastes (e.g. Eccl 8:14) to wrestle with the problem in depth. Most of the laments in the psalter freely admit some guilt, but there are many impassioned pleas for deliverance from undeserved trouble. God is not viewed as a mechanical dealer of justice. The Lord is to intervene because of the psalmists' loyalty and trust, or simply because of the divine mercy (*hesed*).

In a sense, the Old Testament person was in a bind. If the Lord is just, let this justice be shown by the punishment of the wicked, and not negated by the suffering of the just! This thirst for justice had to be sated in this world, the only world where it could be demonstrated. It would be only human to judge one's own condition somewhat leniently in comparison with obvious wrongdoers. But the Lord could not and should not tolerate the rule of injustice; otherwise divine justice is a sham. Hence the Lord "must" intervene—or is the faithful Israelite prepared to recognize that there is a mystery about suffering that goes beyond the obvious standards of justice and injustice? The mystery remains for the Christian as well (cf. Mt 20:1–16).

It would appear that in Psalms 58 and 82 an effort is made to shift the responsibility for a just rule from the Lord to the members of the heavenly court. They are "gods," or "sons of

God" (cf. Ps 29:1), who seem to have responsibility for the administration of justice in the world. Because they fail in their duties, they shall die, just as mortals do:

How long will you judge unjustly
  and favor the cause of the wicked? . . .
I declare: Gods though you be,
  offspring of the Most High, all of you,
Yet like any mortal you shall die;
  like any prince you shall fall (Ps 82:2, 6–7).

The Bible considers the Lord as the primary agent in all that occurs (Am 3:6; Is 45:7). Failure in retribution is not a breakdown of a system that God has set up. Some interpreters have envisioned the moral universe as a tight little mechanical piece: a good deed produces a good result (reward); a bad deed produces a bad result (punishment). There is supposedly an intrinsic connection between deed and consequence. God does not intervene; in the words of one scholar, God is termed a "mid-wife" who supervises this moral order. The view is reflected in Psalm 7:16–17, where the "mechanical" effect of evildoing is described:

They open a hole and dig it deep,
  but fall into the pit they have dug.
Their mischief comes back upon themselves;
  their violence falls on their own heads.

Such passages support what is called the "deed-consequence" theory, the mechanical connection between (good/bad) deed and its consequence (reward/punishment).

But were things really that automatic? Indeed, this "order" seems far from being mechanical. The psalmist has to pray for it to work in Psalm 57:7:

They have dug a pit before me.
  May they fall into it themselves!

Everyone recognizes a certain thrill, an appropriateness to what Shakespeare called "hoist on his own petard" (*Hamlet,* III, iv, 208). But who is so simple-minded as to take this as an "order" of things, that an evil deed inevitably boomerangs back upon the perpetrator?—or that a good deed will bring prosperity with it?

It should also be pointed out that the Lord is portrayed more often in the Bible as one who is *directly* concerned, who intervenes to punish or reward. The psalmists continually express this direct involvement. They apparently did not have to wait long before discovering that the wicked do *not* fall into the hole they dig for the innocent, but the psalmists did wish for "poetic justice," that the wicked *should* fall down instead. It is not with some mechanical order that the psalmists contend. They dare to quarrel with the God of the covenant who bears the responsibility.

d. A Theology of Lament

In the laments of the psalter the quarreling with God is prominent, and one cannot fail to note the extravagant imagery that is used to describe the situation about which the psalmist complains. The reader cannot easily pinpoint the distress of the psalmist. At first this might seem to be a disadvantage. But on second thought we recognize that it is not easy for us to enter into and to identify with the particular sufferings of another. We find it difficult to shed our own concerns, and the troubles of others become remote. Another's personal tale of woe does not trigger the same reaction in us; sympathy is not identity. There is a paradox here. Our ignorance of the precise situation of the psalmist turns out to be an advantage. The very language of the lament is so extreme and broadly pitched that we can fit our problems into the complaint. If the psalmist were very specific about the complaint, we would not often find those specifics applicable to ourselves, and we could lose enthusiasm for the prayer. It is important that we open ourselves to the wide range of images that are used; the imagery and symbols count—the details are beyond us. At times it is easy to identify with sickness (Pss 38:3–5; 41:3, 8) or unjust oppression (Pss 7; 17; 35) or personal sin (Ps 51). But often we cannot grasp the unknown powers which the psalmist faced. Psalm 91 leaves unspecified "the terror of the night," "the pestilence that roams in darkness," "the plague that ravages at noon" (Ps 91:5–6). Moderns also are not spared eerie experiences, or an undefinable hostility. In such cases, the images of the psalms are all the more effective and powerful. Generally the symbols will strike a chord in any human being, as, for example:

> Save me, God,
> for the waters have reached my neck.
> I have sunk into the mire of the deep,
> where there is no foothold.
> I have gone down to the watery depths;
> the flood overwhelms me (Ps 69:2–3).

The most difficult aspect of the language and sentiments voiced in the laments is the note of vengeance and violence—especially directed against the "enemies" that are mentioned so frequently. The issue seems to be all the more exacerbated because one is dealing with poetry that is properly viewed as prayer. How can this be united with a prayerful mood? The situation has been described by E.T. Oakes, S.J. in *America* (March 14, 1992, p. 208): "Many Christians find the Psalms foreign and primitive. They encounter texts that are harsh and unbending, strewn with raw expressions of revenge, of resentment, paranoia and bitterness. The imprecations against one's enemies, many now feel, are too numerous and too bluntly put." To meet this alleged difficulty, there is even a liturgical directive from Rome which has permitted the omission of certain passages from prayer books; one can test this by looking to see if Psalms 137:7–9 and 139:19–22 have been excised. One can understand shortening psalms for liturgical purposes, but when the obvious reason is a kind of censorship—one is not to be disturbed by such vehement feelings during prayer?—the effect is galling, and indeed unfortunate for Christians. The implication could be drawn that "pious thoughts" (whatever these are) are the required material for prayer; anything that is realistic and raw, dealing with the real world in which we live, is to be eliminated. At least the ancients, the Christian fathers, many of whom could recite all 150 psalms from memory, never took that path. They tended to view the enemies as Satan, as the powers of evil, of darkness, which assailed human beings. At times this may seem naive, but as we shall see, that ancient view has some respectable modern counterparts. Such an approach is at least realistic.

The retention of the "scandalous" (as some would say) verses does not mean that the Bible authorizes revenge and retaliation. Nor can one argue that Christian ideals (hardly Christian practice!) leave no room for such realities. That misses the point. Desire for retribution and violence are in fact part of the sinful human condition, and it is better to face up to this in a prayerful and meditative mood than to gloss over it. A few fundamental considerations may be of help.

First of all, there is the frequency and the identity of "enemies" in the psalms. In many cases, the enemies are so described that they are clearly human beings, perhaps people who have harmed the well-being of the psalmist by some action, say an accusation of wrongdoing, whether calumnious or not. Such for example may be the accusers in Psalm 109 (v 3, "with hateful words they surround me, attacking me without cause"). It is helpful to understand the group psychology of a tightly knit unit such as Israelite families and tribes were. One is bound to the community for safety, but if it turns hostile, then it must be somehow warded off—by imprecations. Or it is possible that the psalmist projects imaginary sorrows and troubles onto others; they become the enemy. When we consider even the mild (not necessarily serious) aberrations that occur in modern societies, it is easier to understand how beleaguered the biblical person could feel. They lacked the medical and psychological sophistication available to moderns. It was easier for them to attribute adversity to evil spirits or powers. They knew nothing of medicine and the mysteries of sickness—except that "enemies," or a curse, or some unspecified evil must be the cause of mishaps. Hence we should remember that the frequency and identity of the enemies is not a simple matter.

Second, we must understand the situation of the biblical person, and learn to sympathize. It was not just a question of protecting oneself against wily enemies so difficult to identify. There was also the question of theodicy. Where was God in all this? In the biblical perspective God's justice is celebrated time after time. If evil people flaunt their wickedness (e.g. Ps 73:11, "Does God really know? Does the Most High have any knowledge?"), the Lord cannot leave them unpunished. Otherwise, where is the divine justice? Is God to remain inactive when the poor are oppressed by the wicked (Pss 7:9–10; 14:4; 71:4)? The divine intervention must take place—now, in this life, the only life that the Israelite knows. Hence the agony of Jeremiah in his "confessions"—e.g. Jer 12:1, "Why does the way of the wicked prosper? Why do all the treacherous thrive?" No wonder the psalmist cries out, "My feet all but slipped" (73:2) when he sees the wicked prosper. Let it not be thought that the talion law ("an eye for an eye, a tooth for a tooth," Deut 19:21) was conceived in a crass manner. It represented the very opposite of excess; it called for equity, in which the punishment was adequate to the crime. Thus the excesses of mutually destructive warfare between families and tribes could be averted.

Third, the language is to be understood properly. The very description of hostile machinations has the hue of absolute evil. If one looks realistically at the language of Psalm 22 (placed on the lips of Jesus on the cross), one can only wonder what the psalmist was really suffering from. The abandonment by God would seem to be bad enough; the list goes on: bulls, lions, dogs, the sword, the teeth of the dog, the lion's mouth, the horns of wild bulls, etc. As one commentator has remarked, this could hardly have happened in an entire lifetime, much less on one occasion. Actually, the powerful imagery in these descriptions is an advantage because one need not take these words literally; they are symbols of maximum godlessness and evil that have been unleashed against the psalmist.

One has to become accustomed to the rich imagery that the psalmists use, whether it is a case of being at war (35:1), or being targeted by hunters and trappers (57:7). We have already indicated the woeful condition of the ancient Israelite, who had no medical or psychological knowledge to name a given illness as we have (if that helps us at all); it also explains the wild expressions that are used of nameless evils. Psalm 139 provides an example of the importance of analyzing the language. After an intense meditation upon God's presence and care, the psalmist continues:

> If only you would destroy the wicked, O God,
>   and the bloodthirsty would depart from me!
> Deceitfully they invoke your name;
>   your foes swear faithless oaths.
> Do I not hate, Lord, those who hate you?
>   Those who rise against you, do I not loathe?

With fierce hatred I hate them,
  enemies I count as my own (Ps 139:19–22).

Both the characterization and the rejection of the wicked are clear; they are the object of the psalmist's hatred. Yet these statements have a direct thrust toward fidelity to God: your enemies are my enemies. This is in effect a statement of loyalty. One can object to the ease with which the enemies of God are identified as one's own (a universal human failing!). Biblical language describes this situation in sharp contrasting colors: good and evil, just and unjust, etc. It should be noticed that the ending of this psalm indicates no complacency, but is an admission of weakness and sinfulness:

Probe me, God, know my heart;
  try me, know my concern.
See if my way is crooked,
  then lead me in the ancient paths (Ps 139:23–24).

An important final point should be made. Some will perhaps remain unconvinced by the previous considerations. Feelings of hatred and revenge are simply out of place in their prayers. The uneasiness may stem from the way in which they pray the psalms. The usual way of using the psalter in prayer is to identify with the words of the psalmist. Those words and sentiments, especially when expressing praise and hope, become the vehicle of one's personal aspirations. The difficulty arises in cases where one cannot bring oneself to identify with hatred for others. Is another approach possible? Yes, *hear* the word! Hear the agony and even the sinful violence of human beings—in the context of prayer. These expressions of rage exemplify the demonic in every human heart. Feelings of revenge are not rare or unknown; everyone has experienced them. When they are heard in prayer they serve to illumine our own feelings, and to accuse us of our own failings, our own vengefulness. This is a salutary way of dealing with such psalms. We can and should allow this word of God to judge the violence that lurks in our own hearts. It would be foolish to pass judgment on the psalmist, as if to say "that is not Christian," or "that is not right." Such judgments merely imply for oneself an undeserved compliment, and the real value of the psalm passes over us, wrapped as we are in spiritual "comfort." On this whole problem, see R.E. Murphy, *Psalms, Job* (Philadelphia: Fortress, 1977) 38–46; T. Hobbs and P. Jackson, "The Enemy in the Psalms," *Biblical Theology Bulletin* 21 (1991) 22–29.

We have already mentioned the practice of eliminating certain parts of the psalms for purposes of "piety." There is an unmistakable air of unreality in such a procedure. At stake, too, is a deeper principle: Can we afford to be selective about our biblical canon? In recent scholarly discussions the issue of a canon within the canon has emerged. That is to say, a given book or books become the key to the interpretation of the whole canon and are allowed to snuff out others less "spiritual" or less "popular." This procedure is a doubtful one theologically. It fails to attend to the whole spectrum of the biblical word. In a similar way, the men and women who live in a world marked by violence and revenge should not fail to confront these same realities in the psalms. One of the advantages of the new lectionary that has been adopted in the Roman Catholic liturgy as well as in the lectionaries of other Christian churches is the deliberately wide selection of passages from the entire Bible. It is perhaps inevitable that no choice can satisfy everyone, but the principle is an important one: over a period of a few years one is exposed to selections from the Bible that one might have neglected to read, or would not choose to read. Thus a more comprehensive exposure to the word of God is attained.

This consideration of violence and vengeance in the psalter (as a matter of fact, it occurs throughout the Bible) might appear to make out the laments to be a kind of inferior prayer or psalms. Whatever be the explanation, laments, strong laments, are not generally in vogue in Christianity—except perhaps among the saints. They had a way of speaking forthrightly to God. Teresa of Avila is reported (apparently an apocryphal story, but typical of her) as telling Christ that he had so few friends because he treated them so badly. The fact of the matter is that the laments of the psalter are among the least imitated (perhaps among the least recited by personal choice). The cause of this may be that a lament is understood merely as a complaint, as "whining," or more seriously as contravening the will of God. Christians particularly are prone to recall that Christ urged us to "turn the other cheek," "to forgive our enemies," and so on. In other words, there is a particular image of Christ which governs our freedom of speech in praying to the Father. Yes, what is our image of Jesus Christ? Jesus was not a type of Milquetoast. That is shown by the attribution of Psalm 22 to him on the cross, and in the striking verse from Hebrews 5:7, "In the days of his flesh, Jesus offered up prayers and supplications with loud cries and tears, to the one who was able to save him from death. . . ." There is no inner psychological portrait of Jesus presented in the Gospels, and hence it is difficult to draw specific conclusions. But these words from the Epistle to the Hebrews are strong enough. They do not tell us all we would like to know about the inner feelings of Christ. The only tears we hear of in the Gospels are those shed over the death of Lazarus. The Gospel of John has chosen to portray Jesus meeting his fate without a hint of interior distress (e.g. Jn 18:1–11). The fact that Jesus obediently gave himself over to the Father's will (Lk 22:42) does not eliminate the human pleading which is hardly touched in that line, "Not my will, but thy will." The intimacy between Jesus and his Father is simply not described in sufficiently clear fashion. But the image of Jesus which has been drawn by many Christian writers is misleading insofar as it would eliminate from his mouth the laments of the psalter. This was the prayer book from which he and his followers were nourished. He was not a Stoic; he voiced his feelings. He appreciated more than we do the deep faith and confidence which pervades the laments. As has already been indicated, the path of the psalter is from lament to praise. The genre of intimate lament has all but disappeared from Christian prayer, except when it appears in the psalms, and Christians have much to learn from them.

It has been said more than once that the psalter is a school of prayer—not in the sense that it provides 150 more prayers to add to one's list. Rather, it is the way in which the psalmist approaches God, the personal notes of praise, love, trust that are so frequently sounded. In the midst of all the self-centeredness that characterizes a lament, there are also expressions of love, praise, and trust. Trust is frequently expressed by "taking refuge" (*hasah*). The verb occurs 37 times in the psalms and in the entire Old Testament only 59 times. It will often begin a psalm, as in Psalms 7:2; 11:1; 16:1; 31:2, etc. The implication is not simply that the psalmist has nowhere to turn (which is true), but that the Lord is the only one on whom one can surely rely. Notes of complaint and lament are not allowed to have the last word; these motifs of intimacy with God sweep the reader into a total relationship. The movement of most psalms is from lament to praise. Psalms 39 and 88 seem to be the most forlorn, with little hope expressed. Yet one must realize that these are prayers brought before God, even if in a given instance the psalmist is without enough spirit to voice the confidence which moved him to compose the prayer.

e. Zion and the Messiah

The conquest of Zion, or Jerusalem, was a strategic coup from every point of view. While it was not a very large (Jebusite) city, it was neutral, belonging to none of the tribes. David gave the city its biblical status. In 2 Samuel 5:7 it is referred to as "the stronghold of Zion, now called the City of David." Zion's distinctive religious importance came from David's transferral of the Ark of the Covenant here (cf. 2 Sam 6; Ps 132). When the Temple was built, Zion was understood to be God's "holy mountain" (Ps 2:6), "the city of our God" (Ps 48:21, and also Is 60–62). The heart of its importance is the belief that the Lord had an (earthly) dwelling there (cf. 1 Kgs 8:22–30). Several psalms, essentially hymnic in form, came to be called the "Songs of Zion" (Pss 46, 48, 84, 87 and 122). Two of these can be briefly characterized as pilgrim psalms (Pss 84 and 122). The true home of Israelites, wherever they may be, is Zion, according to Psalm 87. God's protection makes Zion inviolable, as can be seen in Psalms 46, 48 and 76. This Isaianic theme (Is 12:25–27; 33:6; 37:22–32) of inviolability becomes a trap for the inhabitants of Jerusalem against which Jeremiah, about a hundred years later, has to warn them (e.g. Jer 7:1–7). Of course, any religious truth, no matter how exalted in itself, can be abused.

Nonetheless, the presence of God that suffuses the psalms is intimately connected with Zion and the Temple—holy space, because of the presence of the Lord. The problem remains for the modern reader of the psalms to develop a sense of presence, even without the material aid of the Temple. The presence of the Lord was not a static thing. It was achieved through liturgical celebration, or re-presentation. Hence the Lord *appeared,* and delivered oracles of various kinds, such as the theophany in Psalm 50:

Listen, my people, I will speak;
  Israel, I will testify against you.
  God, your God, am I (Ps 50:7).

Intimately connected with the Lord's presence on Mount Zion is the king:

> I myself have installed my king
> on Zion, my holy mountain (Ps 2:6).

The Lord has adopted the king as a son (2:7). At one time this kind of language was written off as merely court style. It is that, but also a lot more because of the divine commitment to the Davidic dynasty that is expressed in 2 Samuel 7. The establishment and cultivation of royalty in the Old Testament is relatively foreign to moderns, even to people who are living in current "kingdoms." It would seem that democracy has become so strong that royalty is merely a figurehead (as may well be the case in Great Britain), but in the ancient world, kingship was taken for granted, and the powers of the king in the ancient Near East were very extensive. It was not just a question of usurpation of power (as also happened), but the light in which the king was viewed. The king was a sacral as well as a political figure. He participated in the liturgy. Thus David acted as priest (2 Sam 6:17–19) and "his sons were priests" (2 Sam 8:18). Solomon also offered sacrifices (1 Kgs 3:3–4), although among the court officials Zadok and Abiathar are mentioned as "priests." It can be stated very directly: the king was viewed as a holy figure, even if he turned out to be an unworthy king. He was looked upon as the "anointed" (the literal meaning of messiah) of the Lord. The significance of this is expressed well by the incident in which David has Saul at his mercy and is urged by his followers to kill him. David stealthily cuts off the corners of Saul's cloak. But he is immediately troubled: "The Lord forbid that I should do this thing to my lord, the Lord's anointed, to raise my hand against him, for he is the

Lord's anointed" (1 Sam 24:1–7). The holiness of the royal person was undeniable.

Hence it is not surprising that many royal psalms were composed. These deal with the currently reigning king, and many of them have been preserved (Pss 2; 18; 20; 21; 45; 72; 89; 101; 110; 132; 144:1–11). Some scholars include many more than these (e.g. Pss 3, 5, etc.). But at least these psalms (proposed by H. Gunkel) are clearly royal. S. Mowinckel introduced the notion of "democratization" of royal psalms, i.e. certain psalms were originally royal, but came to be applied to and used by the average Israelite in the liturgy (e.g. Ps 26). Be that as it may, the clearly royal psalms deal with concrete situations, such as a wedding psalm (Ps 45), and battle psalms (Pss 18, 20, 21(?), 144); a lament over defeat (Ps 89); a thanksgiving (Ps 21). It is likely that Psalms 2, 72, and 110 are to be associated with some royal celebration (coronation or anniversary?). These prayers illustrate the importance of kingship for Israel, but what do they say to the modern reader? Are they just antiquarian notices? The question to be asked is: Why were they preserved? For all intents and purposes, Israel lost the kingship with the fall of Jerusalem in 587. It was the high priesthood that presided over the restored community in the post-exilic era. Nonetheless, the royal psalms were preserved. Why? The most reasonable explanation is that they were reinterpreted as referring to the future. Was this merely wishful thinking? No, because of the divine promise to David in 2 Samuel 7 that he would always have one of his descendants upon the throne in Jerusalem. This promise is clearly reflected in Psalm 89:40, where it is called a *covenant* with David, and it is so referred to again in Psalm 132:11. Royal messianism never faded out in Israel's difficult history. It is nourished by many references in the prophets (e.g. Am 9:11; Hos 3:5; Jer 23:5–6; and especially in the so-called "book of Immanuel," Is 7–11), and thus the hope in a messiah, son of

David, was kept alive. The promise to David was in itself a *dynastic* oracle, referring to David's progeny. Shortly before the Christian era, it was individualized in *the* Messiah, and it is used in this personal way in the Gospels to refer to the Christ (literally, the anointed, or messiah). In fact, the messianism and the hopes of this era are very complex. Contemporary sources speak of two messiahs, and a prophet, and so on. In the New Testament, the title "Son of Man" is favored by Jesus over messiah. It seems that Jesus plays down his role as messiah (the "messianic secret"), because the messiah he intended to be was at cross-purposes with the popular notion, that of a victorious leader who would throw off the yoke of the Romans (see, even among the disciples, the question in Acts 1:6, "Is this the time you will restore the kingdom to Israel?").

The foregoing considerations lead to the conclusion that messianism, strictly taken as *royal* messianism, is not as important from a theological point of view, as it has been made out to be. It appears principally in the infancy narratives (e.g. Mt 1:1; 2:4; Lk 1:32). The followers of Jesus believed that he was *the* Messiah, and they looked to many biblical passages from the Old Testament to confirm this belief. But the acceptance of Jesus was based on more than a genealogical relationship to David. What effect does this have on the royal or "messianic" psalms? We realize that they are not predictions of a future king who will save Israel. They were reinterpreted in that manner by the post-exilic community that preserved them and thus kept their hope alive. But the Christian must realize that in the literal sense these psalms are not prophecies of the future Messiah. They refer to the currently reigning king *in the light of the covenant with David.* The Christian liturgy reinterprets these royal psalms just as the post-exilic Jews did, only it reinterprets them as having come to a completion in the past, in the appearance of Jesus Christ. This is a backward look at prayers which the Christian considers to have been fulfilled in a pre-eminent way in Jesus. Hence they are used in the Christmas liturgy to celebrate the birth of the Messiah in the spirit of the infancy narratives of Matthew and Luke. Relative to the literal historical meaning of the royal psalms, this may be called an accommodation to the liturgical significance of the feast of the Incarnation.

CHAPTER 3

Praying the Psalms

The previous considerations of this Introduction have had a particular purpose; they are oriented toward an enjoyable and productive praying of the psalms. They provide background and hopefully some insights into prayers that seem to be so different from our modern style. The discussion of interpretive approaches and of literary genres is meaningful only if it has contributed to the understanding of these psalms. For we cannot pray what we do not understand. Again we raise the caution that prayer is not learned by a set of rules or by pure information; the way of the Spirit of God has its own short-cuts. But all things being equal, the lessons of history in interpreting and praying the psalms are not to be disregarded. It seems desirable to avoid seizing upon favorite individual lines as ejaculations, while failing to get into the inner movement that the psalms have.

One's prayer style must remain free, without constraint, without prescription. We can all hear a given psalm differently and pray it differently, with equal effect before God. There is no *one* way of prayer. But it would be imprudent to think that the recitation of a psalm, simply because it is part of the Bible, is in itself effective. What good is the traditional Evensong or Vespers, recited or sung by a group as an objective worship of God, if the psalms are not appropriated by the participants? Ideally, the one who prays should truly share in the message of the psalm. We have considered various hermeneutical approaches, and it is left up to the reader to be convinced one way or another. In any case, it is necessary to make a decision in this matter of praying (as opposed to merely mouthing) the psalms.

At least one basic question needs further discussion: How do you pray the psalms? By identifying with the psalmist and the words of the poem? This procedure is natural enough. The words or prayer of the psalmist become yours. That this is not always a simple move has been already made clear in the discussion of vengeance in the psalter. It may also be difficult in other respects as well. Can we identify with a lament when we are in a joyful mood and celebrating? (Normally the liturgy tries to choose particular psalms that will avoid this psychological impasse.) We can hardly allow our prayer to be dictated by subjective moods. A time of joy can be an appropriate time to consider the suffering or difficulties that are expressed in a lament. No legislation can answer this dilemma, but we need to be reminded that we should not be ruled merely by the subjective mood of the present moment.

However, identification is not the only way to "pray" the psalms. Imitating the *lectio divina* (literally, divine reading) of monastic custom, we can meditate on the affections and concepts as they attract us. We can linger over certain phrases, and here the natural poetic parallelism of the Hebrew psalms is an aid. The second (and, in some cases, the third) line of a verse serves to prolong our consideration. It intensifies by repeating the first line. Yet, it is not simple repetition; it is a deepening and extension of it. The first few verses of Psalm 71 (entitled in the *NAB* as a prayer "in time of old age"—cf. vv 9, 18) can serve as an example:

In you, Lord, I take refuge;
  let me never be put to shame.

In your justice rescue and deliver me;
  listen to me and save me!
Be my rock and refuge,
  my secure stronghold;
  for you are my rock and my fortress.

Those who are well acquainted with the psalter will recognize a familiar phrase, "taking refuge in" (God), that has been discussed above. Such a favorite term comes to have a certain coloring or resonance when we hear it so often. In the parallel line a similar idea is expressed, but in a negative way: not to be put to shame. This idea also is frequent in the psalms. Here shame has the nuance of being deserted, despised, ostracized, if the Lord will not provide refuge. The four commands in v 2 are insistent, as it were, to force the Lord to intervene. It is a matter of divine justice, no less. But this justice is not a legal thing; it is the saving justice (recall the concept of the saving righteousness of God in the writings of St. Paul) to which the psalmist appeals. Following upon this insistent demand is a whole series of metaphors that build on the notion of security and refuge expressed already in v 1a. Poetic parallelism offers great opportunities for a prayerful lingering over an expression of trust in God.

Up to this point there is nothing specifically Christian about the prayerful sentiments that have been expressed. The believing Jew will naturally have his or her own coloring and nuance to these verses. And a believing Christian is entitled to go beyond the horizon of the psalmist into the revelation of the New Testament, and to contemplate refuge and protection which Christ affords, the "rock" that he is. This goes beyond the literal historical meaning. The truth is that *anyone*, regardless of religious presuppositions, reads an ancient poetic text with a fuller meaning. This is true of all classics that have deserved preservation down the years. As has been observed before, "If we should really be able to reconstruct the meaning which *Hamlet* held for its contemporary audience, we would merely impoverish it. We would suppress the legitimate meanings which later generations found in *Hamlet*. We would bar the possibility of a new interpretation. This is not a plea for arbitrary subjective misreadings: the problem of a distinction between 'correct' and wrong-headed readings will remain, and will need a solution in every case" (R. Wellek and A. Warren, *Theory of Literature* [Harcourt-Brace & World: New York, 1942] 31).

There are many rich religious ideas occurring in the psalms: trust, hope, praise, love, salvation, and so on. These ideas can be absorbed on their own level (that of the psalmist and the Old Testament world) and then extended into the world of the reader. The reader thus shares in this experience, extending the faith-filled utterance of the psalmist (or even rejecting it?). The lengthening or deepening of the thrust of a psalm or any other Old Testament passage enables the Christian to avoid a too facile allegory or simple substitution of a Christian veneer. We can translate "life" into all that it means for us personally. We know the evils and trials from which, like the psalmist, we wish to be delivered.

The poetic imagery serves this continuity between the Testaments. Certain symbols have an umbrella-like quality. No one who has ever said, "Out of the depths I cry to you"—no matter to whom or what these words are addressed—has failed to be caught up and carried on by the imagery (even if the depths of Sheol were originally intended!). The situation of the reader may very well differ from that of the psalmist, but the images and words cast a wide net that enfolds many varying circumstances.

Continuity is also promoted by the evocative quality of Old Testament poetry. The psalms are not dry dissertations. They are highly emotional summons or outcries that can hardly be muffled, even by a sluggish reader. It is necessary to yield to this movement, to the turmoil of the cries of both lament and praise. This effect must be tested out by the reader—and not once but many times, because there is no one reaction to the psalmic poetry that is final and definitive.

This emphasis upon the continuity between the Old and the New is not meant to be one-sided. There are also discontinuities. The most significant are the laws of legal purity and impurity, which Christians find themselves unable to deal with. However, one should take a long view of this, and look at the purpose, or, better, the symbolism which lurks behind such laws (e.g. Leviticus 19). How meaningful to the average Christian is the use of many sacramentals, such as the sprinkling with holy water, or the wearing of the scapular? Should we not become more aware of symbolism? Kingship and the centrality of Jerusalem are better examples of discontinuity. Perhaps the greatest would seem to be "Sheol," in the light of the doctrine of Christian immortality. But we have seen that there is room in our daily experiences for the "non-life" symbolized by Sheol. The cancellation of the Sabbath by Sunday, the feast of the Resurrection, is another discontinuity, but at the same time one must ask if Christianity has lost something by its neglect of the Sabbath "rest" and the corresponding allotment of time and personal investment of self to the Almighty.

We conclude, then, that there are both continuities and discontinuities in the relationship of the Old Testament to the New. Since the Christian rightly believes that the New is the fulfillment (but not the eradication or supplanting) of the Old, there is a natural temptation to neglect the Old. The ideal is to seek a balance between continuity and discontinuity, or, better, to seek out the continuities which make the Old Testament truly God's word to the Christian. Not too long ago Rudolph Bultmann denied continuity, in the sense that he denied that the Old Testament was God's word for a Christian. Rather, the

Old Testament was bankrupt. Only existentially, from a human point of view, might it prepare a person for Christian faith. This view is profoundly wrong. The Old Testament, in its many levels of meaning, remains the fruitful word of God for a Christian. Contrary to what the famous historian Adolf von Harnack thought, it was not a mistake for the Christian church to retain the Old Testament. No return to Marcion is possible if one is able to open oneself to the religious values that come from the revelation of God to Israel. It is not my purpose or privilege to point out the religious values that come to Judaism. I recognize that they do, but my purpose in this little book is different. It is to underscore continuities and to derive spiritual profit from the discontinuities—all toward a deeper understanding and praying of the psalms.

The assumptions are simple enough. One begins with the assumption that the God and Father of Jesus Christ revealed himself in the Old, and that the psalms witness to this revelation. Further, that the revelation of God in Jesus Christ did not snuff out or obliterate the revelation made to Israel. Therefore it is not a question of a Christian facing a *different* religion in the Old Testament. If there is the same God, there are also continuities, however striking the discontinuities at first sight may seem to be. The reader can be the richer by learning from both.

The modern reader may be somewhat disconcerted by the bold and free way that the early Christians interpreted the Hebrew Scriptures as their "own," in the sense of interpreting them from a distinctively Christian point of view, finding Christ and Christian realities somehow present within the life of Israel and the pages of the Old Testament. It is only in the last few centuries, when "interpretation" or "hermeneutics" emerged with the historical-critical method that the ease with which Christianity absorbed the Old Testament began to be questioned. How is one to respect the historical vision of Israel, and the vision which Christianity has of itself as being fulfillment? How can one be honest to the important and religious values of the Old Testament in themselves, without explicit reference to Christian belief or practice? The intellectual and religious effort to understand the Old Testament within the framework of Christianity is brilliantly described by R.A. Greer in *Early Biblical Interpretation* (Philadelphia: Westminster, 1986, 109–208), to which J.H. Kugel has contributed several valuable chapters on Jewish interpretation.

The Christian interpretation is beautiful and faith-filled, and forms part of the treasure which Christians can draw on for prayer, liturgy, and other expressions of self-understanding. At the same time, one has to be careful of extremes, of exaggerations which fail to appropriate the Old Testament on its own level. Where this occurs, the Christian response to the total word of God is the poorer. There is danger of snuffing out the message of the Old Testament, those books and passages that have no open or pliant reference to the New, but nevertheless remain charged with the spirit of God.

The Christian conscience can be dulled into a lesser degree of morality if it neglects the sharp social message of the prophets (e.g. Amos). True, the Epistle of James contains a striking message on the same topic. But the divine threat uttered through Amos, and actually implemented, can perhaps function more effectively among Christians who may be impervious to the cutting words in James.

Similarly with a purely Christian reading of the psalms. If one wants to pray directly to and about Christ, the New Testament should inform the prayer of the Christian, completed by the striking words of Augustine and the later masters among spiritual writers. But if one is going to use the Old Testament, the Christian must be ready to perceive the provocation and also the enlarged vision of God and reality which is peculiar to it, without its being wrapped up in a Christian blanket.

It is not only a fact, but it is fitting, that the psalter should be recited in public prayer as well as in private devotion. Communal recital calls for a few reflections. Usually this is done by means of alternating the sequence of verses of the choir (or congregation). Another procedure is to have a leader read several verses that are punctuated with some kind of responsorial verse uttered by those in attendance. The method seems to derive from monastic practice, and in its favor one can say that it makes the recitation of the psalms easy and simple; everything can function like clockwork. But that is the trouble. It makes for a mechanical and monotonous recitation. Moreover, when the alternation is simply between consecutive verses, the structure of the psalms is nearly always disturbed, and sometimes totally destroyed. Thus, what should be (or can be) effectively delivered by a solo voice is simply taken up by the group on the other side of the hall. For example, the verses of Psalm 46 (which is the basis of the hymn, "A Mighty Fortress Is Our God") can be run through one after another. But if one attends to the structure, the recitation will take a different form. The structure can and should guide the recitation. Thus, the refrain ("The Lord of hosts is with us . . ." in vv 8 and 12, and probably to be inserted after v 4) cannot be simply treated like any other verse, or the effect of the prayer is diminished. The same is true of the affirmation of v 11: "Be still and confess that I am God!" Such a verse calls for a solo voice, as the structure suggests. It should not be swallowed up by the rush of the opposite side of the choir. It is ironic that the (liturgical) voice of God is dimmed in this and other instances. It is easy to surmise that in Israel's liturgy such key verses were pronounced by one of the Temple personnel in the name of the Lord. So should it be today, in the sense that the divine voice is not simply to be bandied back and forth by a choir. This destroys the power in such psalms as 50:5, 16; 81:7; 82:2, 6; 91:14; 95:8. In other instances, a solo voice is appropriate even when it does not represent the divinity, especially where a leader seems to be giving instructions to a group (e.g. Ps 33:1–3). In some instances the possibilities of several "voices," solo and choral, are many, as in Psalm 32.

The bracing effect of an intelligent analysis and performance in the recital of a psalm can well be illustrated in Psalm 15 (see also Psalm 24). Verse 1 is a clear question; and the remainder of the psalm is an answer (perhaps v 5cd can be separated as a third part). The prescriptions in vv 2–5 are a description of the type of person whom the Lord welcomes. There can be nothing casual about this, nor should the prescriptions be separated. At the heart of the psalm is the integrity demanded in the presence of the all-holy and majestic God. The proclamation of the psalms is to be accompanied by a lively sense of the divine presence and of personal unworthiness. The Muslim custom of removing footwear upon entering a mosque (and imitated by Christians at the church in Taizé, France) is a fitting symbol of what Psalms 15 and 24 are about.

The alternative recitation of the verses in a psalm is common in both Catholic and Protestant tradition, and it seems to derive from monastic custom. It is clear from what has been said above that it is not a happy inheritance. In order to enliven the ritual, the back-and-forth of the verses must yield to a structured presentation. In many cases no one structure is necessarily better than another; either of them, or perhaps a third possibility, is better than the deadening pattern of alternation.

While this Introduction aims at presenting a minimum of presuppositions, scholarly and otherwise, that are helpful to understanding the psalter as a book of the Bible, its main objective is to challenge the reader to *understand* and *absorb* the psalms. It does this by surveying several interpretive approaches and by eventually providing a mini-commentary. But the entire procedure is intended to be explanatory and challenging, not to be prescriptive. The Book of Psalms is perhaps the most read of all the books of the Old Testament. This is astonishing in one sense because the text is very uncertain in many places, the images are distant from our experiences, and the world view is so foreign to the modern mentality. But the psalms have a directness in language; they speak to God and of God—and also to us in our puzzling human nature—and thus they have preserved their popularity down through the centuries. What can we learn about them that will be helpful to a greater understanding? This book has attempted to make suggestions to that end.

The following brief commentary is being joined with the previous pages of introduction in the hope that introduction and comment together will be helpful. Notwithstanding, a note of caution is in order. No commentary, much less these brief notes, can replace the personal struggle to understand the biblical text. This commentary hopes to explain what *needs* explanation. One should go to larger commentaries for full explanations. But most important of all, the student of the psalms should engage the biblical text several times at the outset, *without* looking at this or any other notes or commentary. A commentary is not a repository of "answers"—it is an extension, if you will, of the biblical text. Appropriation of the text by means of several readings makes it easier to appreciate the insights of a commentary, or even better, to write one's own.

PART TWO

A Brief Commentary on the Psalms

Ps 1. This psalm is not a prayer; it is a blessing which has been prefixed in the post-exilic period as an introduction to the book. The theme of the two ways (v 6), good and wicked, is reflected throughout biblical teaching (e.g. Prov 4:18–19; Deut 30:15–19). The metaphor of the fruitful tree, applied to the just (v 3), is familiar from Jeremiah 17:8 and Psalm 92:13–14. Structure: 1–3, way of the just; 4–5, the way of the wicked; 6, the role of God. **1.** A congratulatory formula, "Happy . . ." is typical of wisdom style (Prov 3:13; Pss 32:1; 34:9). **2.** Balancing the negatives in v 1 is the positive trait: continual preoccupation with the Torah (lit. "teaching," and by extension, the Pentateuch; cf. Sir 24:23). **3–4.** The conflicting comparisons: a fruitful tree and useless chaff (cf. Ps 35:5–6). **5.** The "judgment" is probably that pronounced by the community, but it is susceptible of being interpreted as eschatological. **6.** "Way" in the Bible frequently refers to one's manner of life; in Acts 9:2, the first Christians are described as those who belonged to the "Way."

Ps 2. A royal psalm, perhaps composed on the occasion (or anniversary) of the king's accession to the throne in Jerusalem. The exaggerated court style, characteristic of the ancient Near

East, is in accord with the promise to David (2 Sam 7). Structure: 1–3, a description of nations in revolt against the "anointed" (or "messiah," cf. 1 Sam 24:6), the currently reigning king; 4–6, the reaction of the Lord; 7–9, a divine oracle proclaiming the adoptive divine sonship of the king; 10–12, an admonition to rulers to heed the Lord's will. **1–3.** The revolt of vassal nations at the accession of a new king was frequent. But it may be here merely a motif befitting the hyperbole of court style. In the post-exilic period it could be interpreted in an eschatological sense. **4.** The divine laughter is derisive, as in Psalm 59:9. **6.** The choice of the Davidic dynasty and of Zion is a frequent theme in the Old Testament (cf. Ps 132:11–18). **7.** The sonship is adoptive and not mythological, as in Egypt, and not unlike the divine sonship of Mesopotamian kings, except that the Israelite notion is rooted in the divine promise to David in 2 Sam 7, as is also the prospect of world dominion (vv 7–8). **10–12.** The admonition (by the king?) is in the wisdom style ("give heed!"; "perish from the way," cf. Ps 1:6; "Happy," cf. Ps 1:1).

Ps 3. An individual lament attributed to David (as are Pss 3–41); on Absalom, see 2 Samuel 15–16. Structure: 2–3, a complaint addressed to God; 4–7, a trustful affirmation of help from God; 8–9, an appeal and acknowledgment. If this was originally the prayer of the king, it came to be "democratized" and used by the average Israelite. **4–7.** He trusts in the Lord who has always been his protector, a "shield" (Pss 18:3; 28:7); he knows that if he lies down, he will be sure to get up (v 6). **8.** The cry for help may have been separated by an oracle (esp. if translated, "for you have shattered . . ."), assuring the psalmist of deliverance from the enemy. **9.** The invocation upon the community suggests that the prayer was originally by the king, their representative.

Ps 4. An individual lament, which is practically a psalm of trust. Structure: 2, a confident appeal; 3–6, admonition to enemies; 7–9, expression of certainty of having been heard. **2.** *My* *saving God:* lit. "God of my justice," for the Lord shows justice by saving the suppliant. **3.** *You people:* lit. "sons of men," indicating they are only mortal. They are addicted to vanity and falsehood, i.e., to idolatry. **7.** *many:* Those who lack the psalmist's confidence; their murmuring is quoted. For v 7b cf. Numbers 6:25–26. **8.** The joy is comparable to the happiness of the harvest season.

Ps 5. An individual lament. Structure: 2–4, a cry for help; 5–7, the Lord will not tolerate evildoers in the Temple, but (8–9) the psalmist can worship there; 10–11, a plea that the evildoers be punished, but (12–13) the faithful be blessed. **4b.** Lit. "at dawn I prepare (my sacrifice) for you and I wait"; perhaps an oracle from a priest would be given in answer. Prayer "in the morning" is mentioned several times (Pss 46:6; 59:17; 90:14; 143:8). **5–7.** For the exclusion of the sinful, see the entrance torah in Psalms 15:2–5; 24:3–6; only the faithful (vv 8–9) should dare to approach God in the Temple. **10.** The throat is compared to an "open grave" because words of calumny and corruption come forth from it.

Ps. 6. An individual lament, classified among the traditional "penitential" psalms (Pss 6, 32, 38, 51, 102, 130, 143). Structure: 2–4, a complaint and cry for help; 5–6, reasons why the Lord should intervene; 7–8, description of suffering; 9–11, certainty of having been heard. **2.** Apparently a stereotyped formula (Ps 38:2; Jer 10:24) in which divine displeasure and human suffering are associated; sickness was commonly regarded as a sign of sinfulness. **5–6.** God should intervene because of *hesed,* or covenant loyalty, and because after death no one has loving contact with the Lord in Sheol (Pss 30:10; 88:11–13; 115:17; Is 38:18). The psalmist should be kept alive to praise God. **8.** The enemies of the psalmist (cf. "all who do evil" in v 9) are difficult to identify (evil spirits that cause his sickness?). **9–11.** What is the reason for this certainty that "the Lord has heard"? Either these words are recited in the Temple after recovery or they are a reaction to the deliverance promised in an oracle given by one of the Temple personnel.

Ps 7. An individual lament, and more specifically perhaps a "prayer of one unjustly accused." Structure: 2–3, a plea for deliverance; 4–6, a protestation of innocence in the form of an oath; 7–10, an appeal to the just God; 11–14, trust in divine justice; 15–18, punishment for the wicked, but thanksgiving for the Lord's justice. **4–6.** The casuistic style (if, then) is typical of this kind of oath (cf. Job 31). **7–10.** The appeal is made to the Lord as judge of all humans ("assembly of the peoples"); the psalmist can point to a personal innocence which will stand up to the divine scrutiny. **13.** It is not clear in the Hebrew if the subject is God (so the ancient versions) or the wicked person of vv 15–17. **15–17.** These metaphors are familiar in the Old Testament (cf. Job 15:35; Is 59:4; Prov 26:27; Pss 9:16; 28:4): conception that fails to bring forth; falling into the hole one has dug for another; evil recoiling on one's own head. But it is also asserted in the Old Testament that God produced such effects; so retribution is not merely a mechanical correspondence between deed and consequence. **18.** This is, in effect, a vow to offer sacrifice for the deliverance.

Ps 8. A hymn of praise of God as creator (4–5) and of humans as the rulers of creation (6–9). Structure: the two themes are placed in the framework of community praise (2–3, 10; note the refrain or inclusion). **2–3.** The text is corrupt. Perhaps "name" and "majesty" are synonymous with God, who is exalted above all creation. The divine power seems to be all the more evident because of the modest means (infants) that are used. **4–5.** A solo (?) voice proclaims with awe and astonishment that contrast between the divine and the human (cf. Ps 90:1–3). **6–9.** Yet God has subjected all creation to these "mere mortals" (cf. Gen 1:26–28). He has made them little less than *elohim,* i.e. god, or "gods" (Ps 29:1), who are the members of the heavenly court, or angels. Hebrews 2:5–9 transposes v 6 to the new creation in Christ.

Pss 9–10. A thanksgiving song and a lament, united in a very loose structure by an imperfect acrostic pattern (each line begins with successive letters of the alphabet). Praise is proclaimed in the Temple (9:15) by one who acknowledges deliverance (9:4) and who develops the themes of divine judgment and kingship over the peoples (9:5–12, 18–21; 10:16). But there remains the scandal of the arrogant wicked (10:1–11, in the style of the individual lament); God should intervene to save the poor (10:12–18). These two "psalms" should be taken as one composition with the LXX and Vulgate, contrary to the MT. The uncertainty in interpretation comes from the vagueness (unidentified enemies and wicked people) and from the sequence of thanksgiving and lament (but for this cf. Pss 44, 89). **12.** The note of praise is taken up again (cf. vv 2–4). **13.** The "afflicted" (*anawim,* cf. 10:17) are the object of God's "remembering," i.e. active involvement in their favor. **14–15.** The "gates" in Zion are the center of activity in the town, but the "gates" of Death, or Sheol (v 18), serve to imprison the psalmist in the area of non-life; cf. Pss 18:5–6; 30:4. **16–17.** Cf. comment on Ps 7:15–17. **10:2–11.** A description of the contempt the wicked show for God, while they oppress the afflicted. In v 4 the denial of God's existence is a practical one: God does not act. **11.** *shows no concern:* lit. "hide the face"—a frequent motif in the psalms (cf. Pss 30:8; 44:25; 69:18; 88:15; 104:29; etc.); this verse is answered in v 14: God *does* see. **12–15.** This strenuous urging is motivated by the belief expressed in vv 16–18.

Ps 11. A psalm of trust by one who finds refuge with the Lord in the Temple (1, 4, 7). **1.** The command to flee is more probably given by the wicked who persecute the upright (vv 2–3). **4–7.** The reply to vv 1–3 is reliance on the justice of the Lord who "sees" every human being, and punishes the wicked.

In v 7, the just will "see his face," i.e. worship God in the Temple (a common motif; cf. Pss 17:15; 24:6; 27:4, 8, 13; 42:3).

Ps 12. A liturgy of lament which expresses trust in the Lord's word (6–7) for deliverance from the wicked (8–9; cf. vv 2–3, 5). The psalmist seems to voice the prayer of the community (2–5), which speaks in 7–9. **3.** The smooth talkers speak "with a double heart" (lit. "with heart and heart"), or duplicity. **6.** Apparently a divine oracle, uttered by one of the Temple personnel, which inspires the confidence of vv 7–9.

Ps 13. An individual lament. Structure: 2–3, complaint ("how long?" three times); 4–6, confident request. **2.** *hide your face:* see comment on Ps 10:11. **4.** *light to my eyes:* strength and will to live; the eyes are the organ of the body that express life (Ps 19:9) or its opposite (Ps 38:11).

Ps 14 (=Ps 53). A lament that has been preserved in two different forms; see Psalm 53 in the so-called Elohistic psalter. Structure: 1–3, a complaint about "fools"; 4–6, their punishment; 7, a request for Israel. **1.** A practical, not theoretical, atheism is ascribed to the "fool," i.e. the evil person; cf. Ps 10:4. **7.** The reference seems to be to the return from exile (cf. Ps 126:1).

Ps 15. A liturgical entrance psalm (cf. Ps 24:2; Is 33:13–16), or "gate" liturgy, pronounced antiphonally on the occasion of entering the Temple. Structure: 1, question; 2–5, answer. **1.** The question challenges the worthiness of those who would approach God in the Temple (or "tent"). **2–5.** A description of the necessary moral requisites, in word and action. **5.** Interest on a loan (usury) to another Israelite was forbidden (Ex 22:24).

Ps 16. A psalm of trust. Structure: 1–6, a description of the psalmist's loyal relationship to the Lord alone; 7–11, words of trust. **3–4.** The text is uncertain; probably he rejects all gods but the Lord. **5–6.** The metaphors are reminiscent of the partition of the land (cf. Jos 14:1ff; 18:8ff; Ps 142:6). The portion of the Levites was the Lord, not the land (Num 18:20). **10.** Parallel to and synonymous with Sheol is the "Pit" (Ps 30:4; Jon 2:1, 7). The psalmist will be kept alive here on earth to enjoy the fullness of a devoted relationship to God (v 11, "the path to life"; cf. Ps 73:23–28). The verse is applied to Christ's resurrection in an extended meaning (Acts 2:25–31; 13:34–37).

Ps 17. An individual lament. Structure: 1–5, a confident cry, with affirmation of innocence; 6–12, a request to be delivered from beastly enemies; 13–15, renewal of request, with certainty of being heard. **1–5.** The motif of personal righteousness is frequently advanced as a reason for the Lord to intervene (Pss 7:9–11; 18:21–25; etc.). This is not the same as self-righteousness. **9–14.** The enemies are described as though they were lions. **15.** On seeing the face of God (in the Temple), see comment on Ps 11:7.

Ps 18. A royal thanksgiving hymn for victory over enemies; a parallel recension is found in 2 Sam 22:2–51. Structure: 2–4, hymnic introduction; 5–31, the first description, in terms of a theophany, of the king's desperate plight and the Lord's storming intervention to save him on account of his loyalty; 32–49, a second description, more concrete, of the marvelous deliverance in battle by the God who trained the king. **5–6.** The metaphors derive from the ancient myths concerning Sheol/Death; these were conceived as dynamic powers that hunt out human beings, so that even while alive one can be ensnared by Death; cf. Pss 30:4; 89:49. The distress of the psalmist is a form of non-life. **8–16.** In a theophany reminiscent of Exodus 19:16–20, God the warrior fights for the king. **11.** Cf. Ps 68:5. **17.** He is snatched from the "mighty waters," here identified as the human enemy (v 18). **20–28.** The just God recognizes a just cause (v 25) and reacts in kind (v 26). Hence one can rely upon the protection of the Lord who gives "light to the lamp of" (invigorates) the psalmist. **33–46.** The king describes how he was trained by the Lord, and won the battles over his enemies, "foreigners" among them.

Ps 19. A hymn of praise which unites two themes, creation and Torah: 2–7, God's glory in the heavens; 8–11, the wonders of the Law. The connection between them is that the Law reveals the divine will while the divine glory is spoken throughout nature. The final portion (12–15) is a personal reaction: loyalty to the Law, even if there are "unknown faults" (e.g. Lev 5:2–4; Ps 90:8). **2–4.** This could mean that the message is heard clearly by all, or that everyone understands, even if there is no audible sound. **5–7.** Preeminent in the divine handiwork is the sun, boldly compared to a bridegroom (coming forth from the bridal bed where it rests for the night) and to a soldier-giant, as it courses through the heavens. **8–10.** Praise of the Law: each verse relates a characteristic, followed by a good effect. The Torah, as embodied in the Pentateuch, is the expression of God's will for Israel (cf. Ps 119). **14.** The Bible frequently refers to God's role in keeping one from sin (e.g. Is 63:17; Jer 10:13). **15.** This psalm is dedicated to the Lord (cf. Pss 104:34; 119:108).

Ps 20. A royal psalm, requesting victory in battle for the king. The change in person may indicate a solo prayer (2–5, 7–9), with choral responses (6, 10). **2–5.** The king played a central role in the relationship of the people to God; he is the "anointed," and hence a sacred person through whom God blesses them. **7.** Possibly an oracle pronounced by one of the Temple personnel. **8–9.** Victory comes from the Lord, not through human means; cf. Pss 33:16–17; 147:10–11.

Ps 21. A royal psalm, expressing thanksgiving for the many blessings bestowed upon the king. Structure: 2–7, the Lord's goodness to the king; 8 and 14, perhaps choral responses; 9–13, an address to the king, assuring him of victory over his enemies.

Ps 22. An individual lament, ending with a powerful prayer of thanksgiving. The opening words are on the lips of the crucified Jesus (Mt 27:46; Mk 15:34). Structure: 2–22, the complaint, with repeated requests, descriptions of suffering and expressions of confidence (4–6; 10–11); 23–32, a thanksgiving, in which the community is invited to share (23–27), and world-wide worship of the Lord is proclaimed. **4–6.** The meaning of v 4a is uncertain, but the basis of trust is the Lord's past interventions for the people. **8–9.** The sneer and words of the enemies reflect the belief that one who suffers must be a sinner. **13.** Bashan is the Transjordan area east of the sea of Galilee, noted for its lush growth and its cattle (Am 4:1; Ez 39:18); the bulls symbolize the enemies. **15–16.** Symptoms of physical sickness alternate with the wild animals (vv 13–14, 17) in the description of the psalmist's distress. **17.** The MT has "like a lion my hands my feet"; any translation is conjectural. The verse is not quoted in the New Testament. **19.** These actions indicate that the enemies regard death as certain. **20–22.** Note the wide range of metaphors. **23–27.** There is a sharp transition to a thanksgiving ceremony with a congregation (23, 26) in the Temple where the psalmist fulfills the "vows" in gratitude for deliverance. The Lord is acknowledged as rescuer (24–26), and the lowly share in the liturgical banquet (27). **28–29.** The universalism is striking. **30–31.** The text is uncertain, and translations differ markedly. **32.** The future generations will learn of the Lord's display of justice (deliverance) toward the psalmist. Along with other texts, such as the suffering servant of Isaiah 53, this psalm provided the primitive Church an insight into the meaning of Christ's sufferings.

Ps 23. A psalm of trust, structured in two parts: 1–4, God as shepherd; 5–6, God as host. **1.** The Lord as shepherd is a frequent metaphor (Ps 79:13; Is 40:11; Ez 34:15ff). The ancient Orient generally conceived of the king as shepherd, and even as god (Shamash shepherds all who live; *ANET* 387). **2–4.** The vivid terms derived from shepherding cover the contingencies of human life as well: the "rod" for hostile beings, the "staff" for sure guidance. The traditional "valley of the shadow of death" can also be rendered: valley of deep darkness. **5.** This picture of God as table host, perhaps at a sacrificial meal in the

Temple, is all the more impressive because of the enemies who are watching. **6.** In contrast to former enemies, "goodness" and "kindness" now pursue the psalmist.

Ps 24. A processional hymn, with an entrance torah (cf. Ps 15) and liturgy. Structure: 1–2, praise of the creator; 3–6, the entrance torah, question and answer; 7–10, procession (with antiphonal response) of the king of glory into the Temple. The setting in a particular feast remains uncertain. **2.** Sea and river are in frequent parallelism in Hebrew poetry. The Canaanite motif of Baal's victory over *Yam* (Sea, a chaotic power) is reflected in the biblical descriptions of creation; cf. Pss 74:13–15; 89:12–13; Job 7:12; 38:8–11; Is 51:10; Hab 3:8; etc.). **3.** The question asks for the qualifications of the worshipers. Four prerequisites are demanded (cf. Ps 15): freedom from bribery; purity of heart (i.e. a clean conscience, especially as regards neighbors); aversion from idols (lit. what is vain or false); and finally, one should not have harmed others by lying oaths. **5.** Their reward is the Lord's "blessings," a full, prosperous life. **7–10.** The questions and answers continue in antiphonal style, presumably as the Ark (on which the Lord is invisibly enthroned) is carried in procession into the sanctuary. The address to the "gates" remains obscure; see the notes in the revised *NAB*.

Ps 25. An individual lament in acrostic style. The psalmist is a sinner (7) who is hated by enemies and prays for deliverance and guidance. Structure: 1–7, a confident appeal; 8–15, a teaching about the "way" (8–10, 12; cf. vv 4–5), and fear of the Lord (12–14); 16–22, a series of requests. A wisdom influence pervades the poem. **10.** *Faithful love:* lit. "love and constancy" (*hesed we'emet*), the characteristics of the covenant relationship (cf. v 14). **22.** This verse introduces a prayer for Israel, and it is outside of the alphabetical sequence that structures the poem. It is introduced by the letter *pe,* and this seems to be a didactic device to arrive at a 22-line poem (the *waw* verse has been omitted) which spells out the root *'lp* (=teach) in the opening letters of vv 1, 11, 22; cf. also comment on Ps 34.

Ps 26. An individual lament, perhaps by one who has been unjustly accused. Structure: 1–2, request for justice; 3–6, affirmation of innocence; 9–12, request renewed. **4–5.** This negative confession (cf. Job 31) is followed by a ritual of cleansing by water (6–7; cf. Ex 30:17–21). **9–10.** A petition to be saved from the death that is the lot of the sinner; perhaps v 10b refers to the venality of the judges. **12.** A confident vow to offer praise in the beloved Temple (v 8). The affirmation of righteousness (vv 3–8, 11) is frequent in the psalms, and it should be understood as a legitimate denial of guilt, not as an arrogant claim of self-justification (cf. v 11b). "Walk" in vv 1b and 11a form an inclusion.

Ps 27. An individual lament. Structure: 1–6, a poem of trust in God for protection, especially in the Temple; 7–14, the complaint, ending with certainty of being heard (13) and an oracle of encouragement. Although some scholars have claimed that two poems have been combined, trust and complaint are normal parts of a lament. **4.** For this attraction to the Temple, see also Pss 23:6; 26:8. **6.** A vow to offer thanksgiving for the deliverance. **8.** To "seek the face" is to worship God in the Temple (cf. Deut 31:11; Ps 42:3, and comment on Ps 11:7). **13.** The anacoluthon in the MT is striking: "If I were not certain that I should see!" **14.** If this is not a later addition, it can be understood as an encouraging reply addressed to the psalmist.

Ps 28. An individual lament. Structure: 1–2, invocation and plea; 3–5, punishment requested for the wicked; 6–9, thanksgiving and prayer for the king and people. **1.** The "pit" is a frequent synonym for Sheol, or the nether world (see comment on Ps 16:10). **4–5.** The handiwork of the wicked is in contrast to the handiwork of God who will tear them down, never to be rebuilt. **6–7.** A sudden change to thanksgiving, as in many other laments (see comment on Ps 6:9–11). **9.** Cf. Pss 3:9; 29:11, and for the shepherd metaphor ("feed them" is lit. "shepherd them"), see Ps 23:1.

Ps 29. A hymn praising the Lord for various manifestations of divine power. It has been said that the poem (vv 1–10) is an adaptation of an ancient Canaanite (Ugaritic) hymn to Baal, the storm-god. It does describe the course of a storm-god, coming from the Mediterranean across the Lebanon range and into the wilderness of Qadesh to the east. The "voice of the Lord" is the thunder which sounds seven times in this journey. Climactic or "staircase" parallelism (abc–a′b′d) is a feature of both Ugaritic and Hebrew verse. Structure: 1–2, an appeal to the heavenly court to glorify God; 3–9b, description of the journey of the "voice of the Lord"; 9c–10, the acclamation of the heavenly court; 11, a prayer for the people. **1.** "Heavenly beings" (*bene 'elim*) are originally the "Sons of El," the high god of the Canaanite pantheon. These were eventually domesticated as mere members of the heavenly court who provide counsel and service for the Lord (Gen 1:26; 6:2; Job 1:6; Ps 89:6; etc.), and came to be called "angels"; cf. comment on Ps 8:6. It will be recalled that Old Testament monotheism is something that *developed* in Israel. At first there was the recognition that other gods existed, but none could compare with the Lord (Ex 15:11; Deut 3:24; Pss 86:8; 96:4–5; 97:9; etc.). In the post-exilic period a full-fledged monotheism appears. **3.** As often in the Bible, the "voice" is thunder (Ps 68:34; Job 28:26). The "mighty waters" are the "flood" (v 10), the primordial waters conquered at creation (Pss 89:10–13; 93:3–4), over which the Lord is enthroned. **5–9.** Even the majestic cedars (Ps 104:16) are broken and the Lebanon mountain range trembles, as the Lord progresses inland. **10.** The Lord is enthroned as king in the heavenly temple, and receives the adulation of the court. **11.** A prayer for Israel seems to be added here.

Ps 30. A thanksgiving psalm. Structure: 2–4, praise of the Lord for deliverance from death; 5–6, an address to bystanders to share, and to learn from this event; 7–11, a flashback to the days of distress; 12–13, the restoration, and praise of the Lord. **3–4.** The Lord is acknowledged as the rescuer. "Sheol" (normally localized in the belly of the earth as the home of the dead) here stands for the death-like situation that the psalmist was in, and from which he has been brought up by the Lord. There is no praise of God in Sheol; see the comment on Ps 9:14–15. **5–6.** The thanksgiving song regularly appeals to bystanders to join in praise of God. **7–11.** In this flashback the psalmist relives the days of overconfidence, and the prayer that was poured out; see the comment on Ps 6:5–6. **12.** A graphic picture of restoration; sacred dancing was known in Israel (2 Sam 6:16).

Ps 31. This has been classified as a lament and also a thanksgiving; elements of both genres appear. Structure: 2–19, a complaint, with strong overtones of trust; 20–25, a thanksgiving song. **5.** "Net" is a common metaphor for the actions of enemies (e.g. Ps 10:9). **6.** For the hands of God, see v 16 (the hand of the enemy appears in 9 and 16). The "spirit" is the breath of life (Gen 2:7; Ps 104:29–30). **9–14.** In a second phase, the poet again describes the distress in terms suggesting mortal sickness and human hostility. **16.** The "times" (time is something that is filled with action) are in God's hands. **20–25.** In giving testimony, the psalmist also recalls the past in a flashback (v 23), and encourages the Lord's faithful ones. The psalm has many repetitions and echoes from other books. Vv 2–4a are repeated in Ps 71:1–3; for v 13b, see Jer 22:28; for v 14, see Jer 20:10; for v 25, see Ps 27:14.

Ps 32. A prayer of thanksgiving, with overtones of wisdom teaching; one of the seven "penitential" psalms. Structure: 1–2, introductory beatitudes; 3–7, teaching on the benefit of confessing one's sin; 8–9, a divine oracle; 10–11, assurance and exhortation. **1–2.** This is the conclusion to which the psalmist has come, the lesson that is inculcated. Sin is "covered," i.e. removed (cf. v 5). **3–5.** Suffering finally led the psalmist to the realization of wrongdoing and the need to "confess" or acknowledge it before God. **6.** The "waters" are symbolic of the death-like situation threatening sinners (see comment on Ps 18:17). **8–9.** This advice could be conceived as offered by a sage or a priest (perhaps in the name of the Lord, whose "eye"—Ps 33:18—is on the psalmist?). **10–11.** These words to the congregation are characteristic of a thanksgiving song; cf. 31:24–25.

Ps 33. A song of praise to the Lord for the creative word and control of history. Structure: 1–3, hymnic introduction; 4–9, God's creative word; 10–19, God's plan and supervision of humankind; 20–22, an expression of confidence and a prayer. This poem has 22 lines (the number of words in the Hebrew alphabet), but no acrostic sequence. **3.** For "new song," see Pss 96:1; 98:1. **13–15.** For another picture of God's vision of the human race, cf. Is 40:22. **16–17.** See comment on Ps 20:8–9. **18–19.** See also Ps 34:16.

Ps 34. A wisdom psalm, often considered to be a thanksgiving. The acrostic pattern (see comment on Ps 25:22) is quite striking; the *waw* verse is omitted, and 22 lines are created by the addition of a verse that begins with *pe* (thus, a pattern that yields *'lp,* "teach"). The testimony in vv 5–7, which suggests a thanksgiving psalm, is really didactic in character. The reference to 1 Samuel 21:10–15 in the superscription (v 1; it should read Achish, not Abimelech) is not likely. Structure: 2–4, hymnic introduction which anticipates the message of the psalm: the Lord cares for the righteous humble (*anawim*). 5–11. The mention of deliverance (5) develops into a didactic exhortation to trust and fear the Lord (a basic wisdom theme). **8.** For the "angel of the Lord," see Ex 14:19; 23:30. **10.** "Holy ones" refers here to humans, by exception: usually *qadosh* (=holy) is reserved for the members of the heavenly court. **12.** A typical wisdom address (cf. Prov 4:1; 5:7; etc.) introduces a series of admonitions and of maxims favoring the just over the wicked.

The doctrine of retribution follows the optimistic teaching of the Book of Proverbs; the rewards are material ones, signs of God's favor (cf. Ps 37).

Ps 35. An individual lament. Structure: 1–3, invocation; 4–8, imprecations against unjust enemies; 9–10, confidence in coming salvation; 11–16, renewed complaint; 17–18, appeal and promise to offer thanksgiving; 19–26, renewed appeal and imprecations; 27–28, an invitation to friends, the righteous, to join in praising God. The structure illustrates the complexity of this poem. **3.** *I am your salvation:* has the ring of an oracle which the psalmist wants to hear (cf. v 9). **5.** For chaff, cf. Ps 1:4; for the angel of the Lord, see Ps 34:8. **8.** See comment on Ps 7:15ff. **13–14.** Practically an affirmation of innocence, in view of 15–16. **17.** The metaphors of wild animals are characteristic of the lament (cf. Ps 22:13, 17, 22). **21–22.** Note the contrast between what the enemies and the Lord have seen. Similarly, the hostile words of v 25 are balanced by the blessing in the words of v 27.

Ps 36. An individual lament by one who trusts in the Lord's covenant loyalty (*hesed,* 6, 8, 11). Structure: 2–5, a description of the evildoers; 6–10, hymnic statement of confidence in the Lord's protection; 11–13, a request. So understood, the poem can be taken as a unit rather than composite. **2–3.** The MT is obscure. **7.** *Highest mountains:* lit. "mountains of God," a superlative, in contrast to "the mighty deep." **9.** The sustenance given by the Temple is likened to a banquet. **10.** The "light" is the encounter with the Lord in the Temple, the light of God's face (Ps 4:7; 31:17), which enables all to "see light," i.e. to live (Ps 49:20).

Ps 37. A wisdom psalm in acrostic pattern (each letter has two full lines, a stanza). The structure is loose, governed by imperatives (1–8, 27, 34), proverbial sayings (2, 8–9, 16, 21) and the contrast between the just and the wicked (16–40). The writer champions the traditional doctrine of retribution. The just will "possess the land" (3, 9, 11, 22, 27, 29, 34), but the wicked will be "cut off" (9, 22, 28, 34, 38). God rewards and punishes in this life; judgment may be slow, but it will surely come, so one should not be upset over delay (v 1). **2.** *Grass:* Symbolic of the short duration of the prosperity that the evildoer may experience. This common metaphor (Is 40:7) is taken from the rapid desiccation in Palestine caused by the sirocco or the sun. **6.** The divine blessings will manifest the integrity of those who trust in God. **11.** The possession of the land has the overtones of the divine promise (Gen 12:1) fulfilled for Israel (the land belongs to the Lord, Lev 25:23). It is promised to the "meek" or *anawim,* the needy who have only the Lord to rely upon. **16.** This kind of saying is typical of wisdom teaching; cf. Prov 14:16; 16:8; Eccl 5:9. **17.** "Forever," as elsewhere in the Old Testament, has the meaning of indefinite duration, but the idea is capable of expansion into a life that is undying (Wis 1:15) or eternal (John 17:3). **30–31.** This close association of (personified) Wisdom and Law ("teaching," or *torah,* v 31) is found in Sirach 24:23; Baruch 4:1; etc. **35–36.** An example of how insubstantial and transitory is the prosperity of the wicked; it has to be so. This psalm must be held in tension with Psalm 73 and with the Books of Job and Ecclesiastes. It does not affirm that a just order exists (the implication of v 1 is that injustice exists), but it does call for trust in the Lord to bring about such an order.

Ps 38. An individual lament, the third "penitential" psalm. Structure: 2, opening plea; 3–9, complaint and confession of sinfulness; 10–21, expressions of confidence (10, 16–17) and renewed complaint; 22–23, petition. **2.** Cf. Ps 6:2; the psalmist wants to ward off more punishment. The drastic description of the sufferings is stereotypical, as so often in the laments, and there is the usual association of suffering with sin (4–6; cf. Jn 9:2). The description is similar to that of Job: the psalmist is afflicted with "sores" (4, 6, 8), goes about in mourning (7), separated from people (12) who would, of course, regard him as one punished by God for wrongdoing. **14–17.** This "deaf" and "dumb" attitude manifests trust in the Lord alone, whose answer is awaited—a motive to move God to intervene.

Ps 39. An individual lament (3) with wisdom overtones (vv 2, 5–6, 9, 12) and a meditative mood. Structure: 2–4, description of the psalmist's silence; 5–7, an outburst of complaint; 8–12, plea and complaint. **2–4.** The psalmist makes a supreme effort not to sin with the tongue while in front of the wicked; finally the complaint cannot be held back. The reason for this silence is not clear; apostasy? lest the suffering be misinterpreted by the wicked (v 10)? **5–7.** This reflection on the brevity of life cannot be the reason for the silence. It is a frequent topic in the Bible (Ps 90; Job 7:7–10; 9:25–26; 14:1–12; Is 40:6–8), and perhaps it serves here to move the Lord to intervene. **9.** Here the "fool" means the wicked (as often in the wisdom literature); perhaps they used the suffering psalmist as an example of divine indifference (v 10). **12.** *Like a cobweb:* lit. "like a moth." The destructive effect of the moth on clothes seems to be a symbol of the Lord's action with frail human beings. **13.** The tenuous grasp that humans have on life is conveyed by metaphors ("passing stranger," "guest") which describe the first possession of the land by the patriarchs, who were merely resident aliens. **14.** Like Job (7:19), the psalmist asks God to look away. In contrast to Psalm 33:18–19, the divine gaze can be punishing. It is no small virtue of this poem that it ends on a dark note (cf. also Job 7:21; 10:2–22), despite the hope (v 8) in God.

Ps 40. A complex poem of thanksgiving and lament. Many think there are two psalms joined together (2–12; 13–18). Moreover vv 14–18 are reproduced in Psalm 70. Yet praise and thanksgiving are followed by lament in Psalms 9/10, 27, 44, and 89. Structure: 2–4, a description of salvation and its effect; 5–6, a beatitude and praise; 7–11, an acknowledgment of obedience over sacrifice; 12–18, petition and complaint, ending with praise and confidence. **1–4.** The customary direct address (cf.

Ps 30) is here muted to the third person. **5.** It is not clear how this fits into the deliverance that has been described. **7–9.** Obedience to the Law (the "scroll," v 8) is higher than sacrifice (1 Sam 15:22, etc.). **10–11.** There is an unusual emphasis on the psalmist's proclamation of thanksgiving. **12.** If Psalm 40 is one poem, v 12 indicates a relapse into fear of enemies—although hope will prevail (vv 17–18). **14–18.** See Psalm 70; it is impossible to determine which was written first.

Ps 41. An individual lament. Structure: 2–4, introductory beatitude; 5–11, appeal and complaint; 12–13, a statement of confidence. **5.** Those who interpret the psalm as a thanksgiving regard "I said" as a flashback to an earlier complaint. But it can be a prayer that is recited in the present situation. **9.** *Deadly disease:* lit. "A thing of *beliyya'al.*" **10.** *The friend:* lit. "the man of my peace" (cf. Jn 13:18). **13.** The "presence" refers here to the Temple. On "forever," see the comment on Ps 37:17. **14.** The doxology is a later addition, and it closes the Davidic collection (Pss 3–41).

Pss 42–43. An individual lament; the two psalms were originally a single poem (cf., besides the refrain, Pss 42:10 and 43:2, and note the absence of a title for Ps 43). Structure: three stanzas, determined by the refrain in Pss 42:6, 12; 43:5. Complaint is loosely mixed with longing, reminiscence, petition and confidence. **42:2–3.** The psalmist longs to be present in the Temple before ("see the face of") God. **4.** "Where is your God?" (cf. v 11) is a stereotyped question, often addressed by a hostile group (Pss 79:10; 115:2; Mic 7:10). **5.** This happy remembrance serves to emphasize the separation from the Temple, as does v 7, which refers to the mountainous regions of the north. **8.** The roar of the waters suggests chaos and suffering for the psalmist. **43:3.** "Light" and "truth" are personified as guardian spirits to protect the psalmist. Usually it is *hesed* ("kindness") and "truth" that guard the faithful (Pss 25:10; 36:6; 40:11–12; 57:4,

11; etc.), but here light is needed to find the path to the holy mountain of the Temple.

Ps 44. A lament of the community. Structure: 2–9, a hymnic recall of God's deliverance of the people; 10–17, a complaint about the present distress; 18–23, a protestation of innocence; 24–27, the plea for help. The precise historical situation cannot be determined. There is a curious mixture of first person singular (vv 5, 7, 16) and plural (vv 2, 6, 8, 9–15), however that is to be explained (solo voices? role of the king?). **2.** The past salvation history is being recalled to contrast with the present (vv 10–17), just as in Psalm 22 the trust of the fathers in vv 5–6 is in contrast to the suffering of the psalmist in the present. **4–9.** The victory was due to God, and not to the strength of the fathers. **10–17.** The complaint is that the Lord has deserted the people (v 10; cf. Pss 60:12; 108:12). The language is bold and even points out the poor bargain the Lord has made (v 13). **18–23.** As in the individual laments, the motif of innocence is sounded; v 21 grants a hypothetical guilt, only to deny that it would have justified what has happened. **24–27.** An ultimatum is delivered. The sleeping God (cf. Pss 7:7; 35:23; etc.) must now wake up! On "hiding the face," see the comment on Ps 10:11. The divine forgetfulness cannot stand, since Israel did not forget (v 21).

Ps 45. A wedding song for an Israelite king. It is not to be interpreted allegorically, nor can a specific king be identified. Structure: 2, self-presentation by the psalmist; 3–10, praise of the king for his comeliness, virtue, warlike ability; 11–16, admonition to the bride, urging her to wifely devotion, and describing the wedding (apparel and procession); 17–18, concluding address to the king. **2.** The tone and style of the writer suggests that he is a court poet, who presents himself here and also at the end (v 18). The admirable qualities of the king—"splendor," "majesty," "justice"—recall the sacred character of the Israelite monarch; his warlike qualities are also emphasized. **7.** *Your throne, O god, stands forever:* this is addressed to the king; he is called "elohim," or superhuman, just as David was compared to a messenger of "elohim" (2 Sam 14:17ff), or Samuel is termed an "elohim" when he comes up from Sheol (1 Sam 28:13). Because of the king's anointing and relationship to the Lord, he is considered a sacral figure, as it were, something "divine." This appellation is unique in the Old Testament and various other translations have been proposed, e.g. "your divine throne," or "your throne is divine," etc. **8.** Before the so-called Elohistic recension of Psalms 42–83, in which the generic name Elohim replaced the sacred name, the phrase of this verse would have been "*yhwh,* your God." **9–10.** An elaborate description of the wedding; Ophir (in south Arabia or east Africa) was noted for its gold (1 Kgs 10:11, 22). **13–14.** The text is uncertain, but the woman may be from Tyre. **17–18.** An assurance of fertility—the dynasty must continue—and prosperity.

Ps 46. A hymn of praise, one of the Songs of Zion (see Pss 48, 76, 84, 87, 122), which focus on Zion and the Temple where the Lord dwells. There is a clear structure of three strophes, noted by the refrain in vv 8, 12 (and restored by many at the end of v 4). The precise setting in the liturgy (e.g. Mowinckel's feast of the Lord's enthronement) cannot be defined. The songs have characteristic motifs: conquest of the Sea (chaos) and foreign nations, the presence of the paradisal river (v 5). **2–4.** The presence of God (vv 6, 8, 12) is the reason for confidence that chaos (earthquake and raging waters) will not prevail. **5.** The "river" is in contrast to the threatening "waters" and symbolizes God's presence (like "waters of Shiloah" in Is 8:6). The "Most High" (*elyon;* cf. Ps 47:3) is the Canaanite designation of the chief god ("El") in the pantheon, applied here to the Lord. **6.** Perhaps a reference to the answer given to prayer after a night in the Temple (cf. Pss 5:4; 17:3, 15; 90:14; etc.). **9–11.** The marvelous deeds that the community is invited to behold include the divine measures to ensure world peace, and this is implied by the claim to world domination spoken by one of the Temple personnel in the name of the Lord. This psalm was the inspiration of Luther's "Ein' feste Burg ist unser Gott" (anglicized by T. Carlyle, "A safe stronghold is our God still").

Ps 47. A hymn of praise celebrating the enthronement of the Lord as king (whether or not this was a specific feast, as claimed by Mowinckel). See also Pss 93; 96–99. The interpretation of these psalms varies: 1) referring to a specific historical event; 2) referring to eschatological events; 3) referring to a liturgical rehearsal of the Lord's kingship. Structure: 2–6, call to worship Elyon (see comment on Ps 46:5), who "goes up" (in procession to the throne?); 7–10, another call to worship the God of Abraham, with attendance by foreign representatives. **6.** The verb "go up" strongly suggests a cultic rite of enthronement of the Lord (the Ark of the covenant carried in procession?). The trumpet blasts are characteristic of royal enthronement (2 Sam 15:10; 2 Kgs 9:13), when a new king would be proclaimed (2 Kgs 11:12). The enthronement of the Lord need not imply that he was not considered king before; rather, eternal kingship is actualized in the liturgy. **10.** Foreign rulers take part in the celebration; they are called "shields," i.e. guardians (cf. the parallelism in Pss 84:10; 88:19).

Ps 48. A song of Zion (cf. Ps 46). Structure: 2–4, praise of the Lord because of the holy mountain; 5–8, the panic which the sight of the city of God causes to its foes; 9–12, worship in the Temple; 13–15, invitation to the procession round Zion. **2–4.** The city's importance derives from the presence of the Temple; hence Zion is hailed as beautiful, joy of the earth, and as Zaphon (the "north," or Mount Saphon, the Mount Olympus of the Canaanite deities, the Canaanite mythical mountain; cf. Is 14:13; Ez 28:14). It is inviolable and impregnable because God is its citadel (Pss 46:5–8; 76:2–4). **5–12.** As in Pss 2:4–9; 46:7–8, Zion brings panic to the enemy but victory and joyful pride to the people. **8.** Tarshish is unknown, but seagoing ships are meant. **13–15.** The summons to a procession around the city has a message for future descendants. The Hebrew text ends with the enigmatic phrase, *'al mut* (understood by the LXX as "forever").

Ps 49. A wisdom psalm, dealing with the frailty of life and human possessions, and death. Structure: 2–5, introduction; 6–13, a consideration of death, which rules over the wealthy as well as the poor, ending in a kind of refrain (13; cf. 21); 14–21, the wicked and the rich are excluded from God, who cares for the psalmist. **2–5.** A formal introduction to the wisdom teaching about retribution. **6–13.** The rich cannot rely upon their wealth, which they have to leave to others, and it avails nothing in the face of death; both wise and foolish die. **8–9.** The text is uncertain, but it seems that no one can pay off death. Note the contrast between v 8 and v 16. **14–15.** A description of the fate of the wicked; death is their "shepherd" in Sheol. The ending of v 15 is textually uncertain although the MT seems to say that the "upright shall rule" over the wicked—contrary to the customary Old Testament view. **16.** Many understand this as a reference to a future life with God—a deliverance of the just from Sheol by the Lord, who will "take" them as he "took" Enoch (Gen 5:21) and Elijah (2 Kgs 2:9–10); cf. also Ps 73:24 (taking to glory). Then this verse stands in sharp contrast to the inability of anyone to redeem one's self (v 8); only God can do it. Others interpret the verse to mean only that the Lord delivers the psalmist from a premature or threatening death (lit. "the hand of Sheol"). **17–20.** In any case, the fate of the wealthy, who are presumed here to be irredeemable, is to be in Sheol. **21.** There is a deliberate difference from v 13: "not abide" becomes "not understand." But the reason is not clear.

Ps 50. A prophetic liturgy. Structure: 1–6, the Lord appears in a theophany in Zion, and issues a summons to judgment; 7–15, the Lord denies any need of animal sacrifices, since all things belong to God who demands a genuine praise; 16–21, an indictment of the wicked for disobedience to divine commands; 22–23, an admonition concerning thank offerings and loyalty to God. **5.** The issue is sacrifice. **7–13.** The Lord has no interest in merely animal sacrifices; being sovereign (10–12), God needs nothing. **14–15.** But God will respond to genuine praise. **16–21.** Not only formalism in worship, but evildoing is also condemned. Worship is genuine only if the covenant stipulations concerning theft, adultery, etc., are observed; cf. Ps 40:7–9. **22–23.** However, the threat does not foreclose help to those whose sacrifice and way are right.

Ps 51. An individual lament, the fourth and most famous of the "penitential" psalms. There is no historical likelihood that it was uttered by David after his sin with Bathsheba (vv 1–2). Structure: 3–4, appeal for mercy; 5–8, confession of sinfulness; 9–15, request for absolution and renewal; 16–19, a vow to offer praise, but no sacrifice other than a humble contrite heart is needed; 20–21, nevertheless, let Zion be rebuilt for sacrificial worship. It is striking that it is sinfulness, more than sickness (v 10) that weighs the psalmist down. **3–4.** Four requests; the entire lament (9, 12–15) is permeated with the desire to be completely purified of sin (note the metaphors, "wash," "blot out," "purify," etc.). **6.** The admission of sin is explicitly stated, and thus God is exonerated (6cd) from any accusation of unjust treatment of the psalmist. **7.** The sense is that the psalmist is totally sinful, wrong from the beginning. This has nothing to do with intercourse or conception, much less with original sin (which, it will be recalled, is never mentioned by name in the Bible; cf. Gen 8:21; Ps 58:4). **10.** The "sounds of joy and gladness" could refer to an oracle of salvation or to the general thanksgiving sacrifice after one is forgiven. **11.** God's "hiding the face" is here a sign of forgiveness, by contrast with its usual meaning (cf. Pss 69:18; 88:15; etc.). **12–14.** These verses are reminiscent of Jeremiah 31:33–34; Ezekiel 36:26–27. **16.** The psalmist asks to be saved from "bloods," i.e. from death; others understand this plural as indicating bloodguilt (when sinners die in their sin; cf. Ez 3:18–21). **18–19.** An extreme statement, in which the psalmist has become the sacrificial victim: "my sacrifice!" Cf. Pss 40:7; 50:8. **20–21.** Whether or not these verses are a later addition, they are clearly in tension with the spirit of vv 18–19, and indicate the restoration of Temple sacrifice in Jerusalem.

Ps 52. An individual lament? Structure: 2–7, indictment and condemnation of the wicked; 8–9, the reaction of the just; 10–11, confidence and vow. The application to Doeg in the title (2) is contradicted by the mention of the Temple (10). **3–6.** A *gibbor,* or "strong man," is denounced for his plotting and falsehood. **7–9.** The divine punishment will be a justification for the attitude of the righteous toward the downfall of the wicked. **10–11.** Whereas the evil trust in wealth (v 9), the just trust in God's "faithful love" (*hesed*), and will give testimony to the Lord in the Temple.

Ps 53. See Psalm 14, of which this is a variant form, although v 6 (itself an uncertain text) is noticeably different from Ps 14:5–6. The sacred name has been replaced by "God" in this Elohistic psalter (see comment on Ps 45:8).

Ps 54. An individual lament. Structure: 3–5, a cry for help against godless enemies; 6–7, a confident imprecation; 8–9, a vow to offer a thanksgiving sacrifice. **7.** The *lex talionis,* or talion law (a principle of equity in the ancient world, whose aim was to exclude excessive retribution for wrongdoing; cf. Ex 21:23–25), is invoked against the foes; they are to be paid what they intended to inflict on the psalmist (cf. Ps 37:14–15).

Ps 55. An individual lament. The structure is unclear: 3–9, plea and complaint; 10–16, imprecations and complaint; 17–19, confidence in God; 20–22, complaint; 23–24, exhortation and imprecation. **5.** The "death" that assails the psalmist should be interpreted in the broad sense of all his troubles. **7–9.**

No escape can be found from the enemies. **10–16.** Enveloped between two imprecations, the complaint continues about a friend who has turned into an enemy. **16.** As often, Death/Sheol are personified as powers that will take the enemy to themselves. **17–24.** In contrast stands the psalmist's confident assurance that the prayer will be heard. There is a third description of the enemies, followed by a final imprecation (24) and expression of trust.

Ps 56. An individual lament. Structure: 2–3, a cry for help against enemies; 4–5, confidence in God (5, a refrain; cf. 11–12); 6–9, complaint and imprecation; 10–12, confidence. **5.** "Flesh" is the sphere of the human and finite (cf. Is 40:6). **8.** Is the reference to evil people or to foreign nations? If the latter, this may be a royal psalm. **9.** The "vial" is a type of skin-bottle used to contain a liquid; thus the tears of the psalmist are not wasted. On God's "book," see Ps 67:29; Ex 32:32–33. **14.** "The light of the living" is opposed to the darkness of the dead in Sheol (cf. Job 10:22).

Ps 57. An individual lament. Structure: 2–4, a confident plea; 5–7, a complaint, interrupted by the refrain in v 6; 8–11, vow to offer thanksgiving, ending in the refrain (12). Verses 8–12 are to be found in Psalm 108:2–6, where they introduce a complaint (itself apparently taken from Psalm 60:9–14). **4.** The Lord's "love and fidelity" are guardians sent to protect the psalmist (cf. v 11 and comment on Ps 43:3). **7.** The enemy should fall into its own trap (cf. Pss 7:16–17; 9:16; etc.). **9.** "Waking the dawn" has many parallels from Ovid to Shakespeare and beyond. **11.** Cf. Ps 36:6.

Ps 58. A lament (?). The problem here is: Who is being addressed? The enigmatic *elem* in v 2 is usually changed to *elim,* gods or divine beings, the members of the heavenly court (cf. Ps 29:1 and see Ps 82, where the Lord rebukes the "gods"). Then the implication of the psalm is that they do not live up to their responsibilities for the maintenance of justice. Some would claim that the *elim* here means human authorities, on the basis of Ex 4:16, 7:1; Ps 45:7; Zech 12:8. Hence this psalm could refer to human authorities who abuse their power. Structure: 2–3, accusation of the responsible powers; 4–6, description of the activities of the wicked; 7–10, imprecation; 11–12, divine vengeance for the oppressed. **2.** The meaning of *'lm* (gods or powerful ones) determines the direction of the exegesis: either the lesser divinities or human authorities are being accused for delinquency in the administration of justice. **4.** The activities of the "wicked" are set off against the situation of the "just" (v 11). They are described vividly: corrupt since birth (cf. Ps 51:7), and like a poisonous snake which cannot be charmed because it is deaf. **9–10.** The meaning of these verses is uncertain. If the snail is referred to, it leaves a trail of empty shells, and hence "melts away." **11.** Washing one's feet in the blood of the wicked is a gesture of revenge (cf. Ps 68:24; Is 63:3–6). **12.** One cannot doubt that ultimately there is a divine justice.

Ps 59. An individual lament. Although it has nothing to do with David (the superscription in v 1), some claim that the poem originally referred to a king. Refrains abound: vv 7 and 15; and the poem is divided by the refrain in vv 10–11a (cf. v 18) into two parts which contain pleas, complaints and imprecations, with a thanksgiving hymn at the end (vv 17–18). **9.** For the derisive laughter of God, see Pss 2:4–5; 48:6.

Ps 60. A lament of the nation. Despite the title which associates the poem with David's wars (v 1; cf 2 Sam 8), the precise occasion is unknown. A serious defeat, perhaps at the hand of Edom (v 11), has occurred. Structure: 3–7, complaint and appeal; 8–11, the divine response; 12–14, complaint and confidence. Note that vv 7–14 are to be found in Ps 108:7–14. **3–5.** The Lord is directly accused of harsh treatment of his own people. **8–11.** In the divine response the Lord claims sovereignty over several areas—over Israel and Judah and the traditional enemies (v 10). The question in v 11 seems to indicate that God expects cooperation from the people in re-establishing sovereignty, but cf. Ps 108:11. The oracle of salvation (vv 8–11) is sandwiched in between two complaints, but the poem ends on a confident note.

Ps 61. An individual lament, but vv 7–8 would suggest a royal psalm. Structure: 2–3, invocation; 4–5, confident expectation; 6–9, between certainty that the praise is heard (6) and a vow (9) is a prayer for the king (7–8). **3–5.** The psalmist is in a death-like situation, and asks for the presence of God in the Temple (5). **8.** For "love and fidelity," see comment on Ps 57:4.

Ps 62. A psalm of trust. Structure: 2–5, affirmation of trust, despite enemies; 6–9, appeal to the congregation to trust; 10–11, admonition about human mortality and greed; 12–13, a numerical saying. **2.** The refrain in vv 2–3 and 6–7 uses metaphors that are frequent in psalms (18:3; 27:1; etc.). **4.** Words addressed to enemies of the psalmist. **10.** The brevity of human life is a common biblical theme; cf. Pss 39:5–7; 90:3–10; 144:4. **12–13a.** This seems to be a divine oracle, cast in the form of a numerical saying (common in wisdom literature; cf. Prov. 6:16ff; 30:15ff) which points to the divine power and *hesed*.

Ps 63. A lament that is dominated by trust. The psalmist is filled with a desire for the presence of God in the Temple (cf. Pss 42–43). Structure: 2–4, a strong yearning; 5–9, a description of the joys of God's presence; 10–11, imprecations and prayer. **4.** The divine *hesed* or "love" is valued beyond life itself. **10.** *depths of the earth:* where Sheol was localized. **11.** *prey of jackals:* and presumably deprived of burial, a terrible fate for the ancients. **12.** *the king:* perhaps this was originally a royal psalm that came to be "democratized" and used by all.

Ps 64. An individual lament. Structure: 2–3, a cry for help; 4–7, a description of the enemies' attack; 8–9, the divine intervention; 10–11, thanksgiving. **4.** "Swords" and "arrows" are a frequent metaphor (Pss 57:5; 120:2–4), probably for calumny. But the arrows in v 8 are divine, in retaliation, as their own tongues destroy the evildoers (v 9). **10.** The work of God ("God's deed"), which Qoheleth (Eccl 3:11; 8:17; 11:5) found so mysterious, is plainly perceived, and hence praised (11).

Ps 65. A song of praise. The Lord is praised as one who pardons and blesses, as creator, and especially as the one who bestows rain and fertility on the land. Structure: 2–5, the reasons for praising God in the Temple; 6–9, a creation hymn addressed to the "savior"; 10–14, the Lord's granting of fertility. **3.** *All flesh:* Israelites especially; they confess their sins to the Lord (4), and are chosen to worship in the Temple (5). **6.** God's "awesome" deeds, which usually refer to saving works, indicate here (and in Ps 139:14) the work of creation (7–8). **9.** There is an unusual mixture of fear and joy on the part of the distant inhabitants. **10–14.** The description of the divine preparation of the land (10–11) becomes exuberant in 12–14; wagon-wheel tracks are left by the Lord's chariot as it travels in the rains that fructify the earth; joy girds the hills, and the fields and valleys sing!

Ps 66. A mixed type. A collective thanksgiving song (1–12) is followed by an individual thanksgiving (13–20). The relationship between the two parts is not clear (unless the individual is a king or some representative who speaks for the people). The prayer has accents of universalism (1, 4, 7–8), and v 1 is found again in Pss 98:4, 100:1. Structure: 1–4, invitation to praise God; 4–8, a description of the awesome deeds of God, to be hailed by all; 9–12, the divine testing (perhaps recent events) of the people; 13–15, a declaration of a thanksgiving sacrifice; 16–20, a typical address to the bystanders giving testimony to the Lord's intervention. **5.** The invitation seems to imply that something concrete is seen; see also Pss 46:9. **5–6.** In contrast to Ps 65:6 the "awesome" deeds are the saving events at the Red Sea and the river Jordan; cf. Ps 114:3. **10.** The testing (a prominent biblical theme; cf. Gen 22:1; Deut 8:2, 16; Ps 26:2) is only alluded to by the figure of "fire and water" (v 12; cf. Is 43:2). **15.** The vow once made is now being fulfilled, and testimony is given, with emphasis on innocence (v 18; cf. Ps 26:1–8).

Ps 67. The genre of this prayer turns on the understanding of vv 7–8: are they a prayer (for a rich harvest; cf. *NJV*), or a statement (in thanksgiving for the harvest; cf. *NAB, NEB*)? Structure: There are two petitions (2–4 and 5–6) and a conclusion in vv 7–8. There is a refrain in vv 4 and 6, but it is noticeably absent after v 8. **2.** A restatement of the blessing of Aaron (Num 6:24–26; cf. also Pss 4:7–8; 31:17). **3.** God's "rule" and "saving power" in this context is the fertility of the land that should be seen by "all the peoples" as reason to praise God. The universalism in this poem is noteworthy.

Ps 68. A hymn of praise (?). This poem is very obscure. It has been called a collection of incipits (opening lines of various songs; so W.F. Albright). If it is a song of praise, it has no particular structure, and in many places the translation is uncertain. **2.** A comparison with Numbers 10:3 suggests that the Ark is being carried in procession. **5.** "Cloud-rider" is a standard epithet of Baal in the Ugaritic literature, and is appropriated to the Lord; cf. v 34; Deut 33:26; Is 19:1; Ps 18:10–11. **8–11.** A description of the Lord's coming in a theophany (cf. Jgs 5:4–5). **12–19.** Perhaps a description of military victory (achieved by the Almighty, 15), and of eventual residence of the Lord on the chosen mountain (instead of the apparently hostile and perhaps "jealous" mountains of Bashan). **20–24.** Thanks to the Lord, the people are delivered. **25–28.** A procession into the sanctuary is described; it is not known why these specific tribes are mentioned. **29–32.** God's power is invoked against enemies, primarily Egypt, and tribute from the nations will be exacted (but this seems to lead to conversion; cf. v 33). **34.** See comment on v 5.

Ps 69. An individual lament. Structure: Cries for help and descriptions of misery alternate through vv 2–30; 31–37, a vow to offer thanksgiving and a prayer for Zion. The psalmist is sick (27, 30) unto death (2–3, 15–16), and persecuted by enemies as a thief (4–5) and as one smitten by God (9–10, 19–20). With Psalm 22, this prayer is most frequently quoted in the New Testament in relation to Christ's suffering. Like Psalm 22 it can be regarded as a description of the exemplary suffering of an innocent person who relies upon God for deliverance—applicable therefore to the Son of Man. **2–3.** The "waters" are taken up again in vv 15–16 with other synonyms for Sheol, which exercises its power over the psalmist. **5–7.** Although sinfulness is admitted, the suffering is unfair, and appeals are made to the Lord to intervene for the sake of those who look to God and who would be scandalized at the unjust suffering. **13.** Everyone—the elders who sit at the gate to administer justice, and even drunkards—makes sport of the psalmist. **15–16.** Cf. vv 2–3. **18.** Cf. comment on Ps 10:11. **22.** While food and drink may refer to the practice of giving a meal to unfortunates, the persecutors give gall and vinegar; cf. Mk 15:23 and parallels. **22–29.** A series of imprecations that culminate with the wish that the enemies' names be blotted from the "book of the living" (cf. Pss 56:9; 139:16). **33–35.** This is the lesson that the "lowly ones" (*anawim*) are to learn from the deliverance the Lord will effect. **36–37.** Perhaps an addition, although the author could easily pass from the individual to the group; it presupposes the destruction of the kingdom of Judah (587).

Ps 70. An individual lament, almost identical with Psalm 40:14–18. The description of the psalmist's distress is vague, and has to be inferred from the imprecations in 3–4. Some have argued that Psalm 70 was supposed to be read with Psalm 71, which lacks a superscription or title.

Ps 71. An individual lament. The so-called anthological style characterizes the composition; it is made up of several expressions borrowed from other psalms (cf. Pss 31:2–4; 22:10–11). This is the prayer of a sick, persecuted person, now old (9, 18), who in the past experienced divine protection but now despairs over attack from "enemies" (7, 10–13). The psalmist affirms hope and trust, and promises to proclaim God's "mighty works" (16). The structure is rather loose: 1–8, a plea to be delivered from "the power of the wicked," followed by expressions of trust, and praise; 9–16, a complaint about the enemy, concluding with a vow to praise God. There is a fairly consistent alternating of request, confidence and motifs of trust and vow; it ends with the certainty that God has heard the request. **2–3.** Cf. Ps 31:2–4. **5–6.** For this motif, see Ps 22:10–11. **7.** A "portent" here is one on whom God's anger has been poured out (cf. v 11, and also Deut 28:46 for *mofet* as a punishment). **12–13.** Cf. Ps 70:2–3. **15.** Note the insistence on proclaiming the Lord's "justice" (15, 16, 19, 24), i.e. the deliverance of the psalmist.

Ps 72. A royal psalm, perhaps composed on the occasion of the coronation of a new king in Jerusalem. The king is a descendant of David (but hardly the "Solomon" of the title), and the dynastic oracle of 2 Samuel 7 forms the basis of the high hopes held out for his rule: justice, peace, life forever, and worldwide rule. The courtly style of exaggeration is not merely an imitation of foreign courts; the justification lies in the divine plans for the Davidic dynasty. The king's reign is described in "messianic" language; the currently reigning king is seen in the light of the national hopes for the dynasty. The atmosphere of the prayer is not a declaration of fact so much as wishes that the king will fulfill this tableau. Structure: 1–4, a just reign; 5–7, a long and beneficent reign; 8–11, a worldwide reign; 12–15, royal concern for the poor; 16–17, a prayer for royal prosperity. **1.** The parallelism indicates that the "king" is of royal lineage, and not a usurper. He is to be given the divine gift of "justice" for his rule, a common ideal for the kings of the ancient Orient (e.g. Hammurabi; cf. *ANET* 164, 177–78). **3.** For this kind of hyperbole, see Is 32:15–20. **8.** Cf. Zech 9:10. The worldwide rule seems to extend from the Mediterranean to the Persian Gulf and from the Euphrates (the "River") to the "ends of the earth" (perhaps the Mediterranean islands). **9.** Cf. Mic 7:17; Is 49:23.

14b. Literally, "precious is their blood in his sight"; i.e. he will not allow their blood to be shed; he will not allow them to be oppressed; cf. Ps 116:15. **17.** There seems to be an allusion to Genesis 12:3 and other passages where Abraham is said to be a source of blessing for all nations. **18–19.** The collection of the Second Book of Psalms (cf. Ps 41:14) ends with this doxology, and v 20 probably indicates the close of a collection of Davidic psalms (Pss 51–70).

Ps 73. A thanksgiving psalm, opening the Asaph collection (Pss 73–83; 50); Asaph is mentioned in Ezr 2:41 as an ancestor of the Temple singers. The genre is thanksgiving, although the poem picks up on a wisdom theme, like Psalm 49, the problem of retribution; the poet describes a personal crisis, but only after stating the conclusion about God's goodness (v 1 and in greater detail in vv 23–27, which ends with an avowal of thanksgiving in v 28). Structure: 1–3, introduction; 3–12, a description of the prosperity of the wicked; 13–17, the doubts of the psalmist; 18–22, the fate of the wicked; 23–28, the fate of the psalmist. **1.** This is a conclusion which was reached only after much trial (vv 2–3, with the statement of the problem). Although MT and the ancient versions read "Israel" (*lyśr'l*), many prefer the emendation "to the upright" (*lyšr 'l*). **9.** Perhaps the wicked speak blasphemously ("their mouths in heaven"); cf. v 11. **13b.** A reference to the liturgical act of purification (Deut 21:6). **17.** In the Temple the psalmist meditates on the "after" (*aharit*) of the wicked, which is then described in the traditional terminology of the wisdom teachers; there is nothing unusual about these conclusions, despite the Temple meditation. **23–28.** These verses present the psalmist's insight into the lot of the just, which is to be found in companionship with God (25, 26, 28); this is "my good" (28). Does v 24 indicate that the association with God goes beyond death, "in glory"? Many argue that it does, citing the technical use of the term *lqh* (so Elijah in 2 Kgs 2:1ff, and Enoch in Gen 5:24, who were "taken"; cf. Ps 49:16). The terms "always" and "forever" do not settle the question; these words in Hebrew do not have the nuance of infinity but merely indefinite duration. In v 25 "heaven" is above the firmament, physical space, in contrast to the "earth." Others argue that these lines indicate only that the psalmist is delivered from evil and impending death. In any case, these verses provide one of the most sublime and beautiful descriptions of a personal relationship to God.

Ps 74. A lament of the community, on the occasion of a destruction of the Temple (probably 587). Structure: 1–11, a complaint and description of the situation; 12–17, a hymn in praise of God's power in creation; 18–23, a second appeal to God. After the initial "why?" come two lengthy appeals introduced by "remember." These are separated by the creation hymn which itself serves as a reminder to the Lord of the divine power which should be used in Israel's honor. **2–4.** Such terms as "your flock," "Zion, where you dwell," are highly charged and are designed to induce the Lord to intervene; so also the mention of the presence of the military signs of the enemy in the Temple itself. **9.** Here the (absent) "signs" are some kind of message from the Lord, but the prophets are mute. **12–17.** Creation is considered one of the "saving deeds" or "victories" (v 12), and it is presented in terms of the mythical primordial battle between the Lord and chaos (represented by *Yam,* or Sea; the "dragons"; the "heads of Leviathan," as in Is 27:1; Ps 104:26). There can be no question that the Lord is powerful; but will there be action? **18–23.** The treatment of Israel is portrayed as an insult to the Lord's honor; let the covenant be brought into play! Israel's "cause" (v 22) has become the cause of God.

Ps 75. A "liturgy" (?). The classification is very uncertain, and there seems to be a mixture of genres. Both the community and an individual speak praise; and a solo voice delivers an oracle of judgment. Structure: 2, introduction by the community; 3–4, a divine oracle; 5–9, a warning to the community;

11–12, an announcement of praise and victory. **2.** The "wondrous deeds" in this context are the Lord's just judgments upon malefactors. **3–4.** A divine oracle, proclaiming judgment, by the creator (v 4). **5–9.** These prohibitions are warnings that urge submission to the "Rock." The cup (of wrath) is a frequent metaphor (Is 51:17; Jer 25:15). The particular wrongdoing seems to be hubris (vv 5–6). **10–11.** It is difficult to identify the speaker with the community, but see v 2. **11.** Perhaps a priest, who would have delivered the oracle of vv 3–4, speaks here.

Ps 76. A hymn of praise, or song of Zion (cf. Pss 46, 48). Structure: 2–4, an acknowledgment of the Lord's protective dwelling in Zion; 5–11, a description of victory over Zion's enemies; 12–13, an encouragement to fulfill vows to the Lord. The interpretation is open-ended: Is the battle (vv 5–10) an historical, eschatological or cultic event? It seems more probable that originally the poem served to re-present the Lord's saving deed in the liturgy—not without a certain orientation toward the future (11–13). **3.** *Salem:* an older name of Jerusalem (Gen 14:18). **4.** See Ps 46:10 for the motif of the divine breaking of weapons; this suggests that the victory is achieved by the Lord alone. This is more a generalization about Zion's inviolability than a reference to a particular battle; the description continues through v 10, with the theophany described in v 5. **6–8.** The sleep of the vanquished is not necessarily death, but torpor and daze; they are silenced by the sight of the "awesome" (vv 5, 8, 13) one. **11–12.** The text is obscure, but it seems to indicate fulfillment of vows to the Lord.

Ps 77. An individual lament (2–11) and a hymn of praise (14–21). Even if the hymn is an addition, it supplements vv 12–13 which serve as a transition. The psalmist laments (as a representative?) over the sad situation of the people, abandoned by God—an unusual subject for an individual lament. Then (v 12) consolation is derived from the memory of the ancient salvation history, which is pondered and related. **2–11.**

After a long description of misery and brooding, the cause is finally revealed: the Lord seems to have rejected the people (by the changing of the "right hand," v 11; cf. Ps 78:54; or the "arm," v 16, which had saved Israel in the past). **8–10.** These questions reflect upon the great confession of Exodus 34:6 (cf. also Pss 86:5; 145:8); does that confession still ring true? **14–16.** A hymn begins, recalling the events of the Exodus. The "holiness" of God's way (v 14a) is not meant in an ethical sense; God is different, mysterious and hence incomparable (v 14b); cf. Ex 15:11. **16.** *Your people:* those who were rescued from Egypt, the children of Jacob and Joseph (cf. v 21). **17.** The crossing of the Red Sea is described in terms of a victory over the primordial waters by the God of thunder and lightning who comes through the sea (cf. Hab 3:15) without leaving a trace. The ending is somewhat abrupt; as it stands, the entire poem can be seen as a reflection of the community, and not simply of one individual.

Ps 78. An historical psalm (cf. Pss 105, 106) in the style of a hymn, showing considerable wisdom influence. Structure: 1–11, introduction; 12–72, historical illustration of the continual infidelity and disobedience of Israel, and the continual forgiving response of the Lord (punishing but also saving his people) from the Exodus to the time of David. There is a delicate mixture of pedagogy and history, as the writer chronicles the twists and turns of the past. As the notes in the revised *NAB* psalms indicate, this historical meditation can be divided into the wilderness events (12–39), and the movement from Egypt to Canaan (40–72). **1–11.** The introduction is composed in the wisdom style (cf. Ps 49:1–5; Prov 3:1; 5:1); history will be used as a lesson, as the comments (almost like refrains) in vv 17, 32, 40 and 56 demonstrate. **5.** The reference is to Exodus 10:2 and Deuteronomy 4:9: the handing down of the sacred tradition (Deut 32:7). **6–8.** The instruction of future generations is also the purpose of this psalm; they are not to "forget," but to "remember" (vv 7, 11, 35, 39, 42). **9.** The reference to Ephraim is sudden and puzzling. This was the most important tribe in the north, and it is singled out in v 67 as the tribe the Lord did not choose; but it is not clear why it merits first mention (vv 9–11) in the history which really begins in v 12. The "day of battle" is hard to explain. **12.** Zoan is identified with Tanis, the Hyksos capital in the Nile delta, which is not mentioned in the Exodus narrative. In 13–16 is a description of the traditional events associated with the crossing of the Sea and the traversing of the desert (pillar of cloud, miraculous water, etc.). Israel's rebellion (17–19) is met by the Lord's over-generous supply of quail and manna (23–29), which "killed their best warriors." The episode of Kibroth-hattaavah (Num 11:34) is dramatically described in 30–31. The death of the desert generation (33–34) leads into a portrayal of Israelite infidelity and divine forgiveness. The ingratitude is made all the more impressive by the description of the plagues and the deliverance from Egypt in vv 40–53. (The number of plagues is seven, in contrast to the ten of Exodus 7–12; see also Ps 105:27–38.) This culminates in the conquest of the "holy land" (54–55). Israel's infidelity (56–59) is the reason for the victories of the Philistines who captured the Ark and destroyed Shiloh (60–64). In a bold metaphor (65) the Lord is compared to a warrior who shakes off the effect of wine and fights victoriously. Ephraim is rejected (cf. vv 7–9), but the Lord chooses Judah, Zion and David (67–70), a theme dear to the Deuteronomist school (cf. 1 Kgs 8:15–16). In contrast to other surveys of salvation history (e.g. Ps 105), this poem includes Zion and David as the culminating events.

Ps 79. A lament of the community (cf. Ps 74) over some unnamed disaster; cf. v 1, the defilement of the Temple (587? certainly not as late as the Maccabean period). Structure: 1–4, the complaint; 5–10, several pleas, with motifs to move the Lord to intervene; 11–13, final plea and vow to give thanks. **2–3.** This highly charged description is taken up in 1 Maccabees 7:17.

Lack of burial was felt to be a terrible plight (Deut 28:26). **5–10.** While Israel's guilt is not denied, the "nations" are described so as to move the Lord. God has to act "for the glory of your name" (cf. Ps 74:18–20). **12.** The retaliation is to be, literally, "sevenfold into their bosoms"—an expression derived from the ample folds of the outer garments that served as a receptacle, and hence an appropriate metaphor for full punishment.

Ps 80. A lament of the community. The occasion and date cannot be determined. Note the refrains in vv 4, 8, 20. Structure: 2–4, a cry for help; 5–8, the present evils; 9–12, the contrast with the past history; 13–16, an appeal; 17–20, imprecation and confident appeal. **1.** *shepherd:* see Gen 48:15; 49:24; Ps 77:21. **2.** The mention of the northern tribes suggests a northern origin (the troubles of 734–31, or the period of Josiah?). The Lord was conceived as invisibly enthroned "upon the cherubim," the mythical winged figures, half-human and half-animal, associated with the Ark as protective genii. **4.** For the light of God's face, cf. Num 5:26. **6.** "The bread of tears": cf. Job 3:24, where Job's groaning is his "bread." **9.** For the figure of the vine for Israel, see Hos 10:1; Is 5:1–7; 27:2–6; Ez 17. **11.** The "cedars of God" are giant trees that, like "mountains of God" (36:7), are exclusively the work of God. **12.** For the sea and the river, see the comment on Ps 72:8. **16b.** If this verse is genuine (cf. v 18 and the textual notes of the revised *NAB*), it refers to the reigning king, who sits at the Lord's "right hand" (Ps 110:1). **18.** *the one:* lit. "a son of man," a phrase that designates merely a human being.

Ps 81. A prophetic liturgy (cf. Ps 50). Jewish tradition associates it with the Feast of Tabernacles, and on the basis of its similarity to Psalm 95, Mowinckel includes it in the enthronement psalms. Structure: 2–6b, hymnic introduction; 6c–17, an oracle delivered in the name of the Lord, perhaps by a prophet. For other examples of oracles, cf. Pss 12:6; 32:8–9; 50:7ff. **3–4.** Musical accompaniment is customary (Ps 150:3–4); cf. Lev 23:24, 34, for the trumpet on the solemn feast. **6c.** The divine message, in the first person, follows. **7–8.** The Lord freed Israel from slavery (the "basket" is for carrying clay bricks, as at the time of the Exodus), and appeared in "thunder" at Sinai. **10–11.** Cf. Ex 20:2–3 and the comment on Ps 29:1 concerning monotheism. **12–15.** For the warning, cf. Ps 95:8–11. **17.** See v 11 and also Deut 32:13–14.

Ps 82. The genre of this psalm is not clear, perhaps a prophetic liturgy. In a courtroom scene, God accuses the "gods" (or elohim beings who belong to the heavenly court) of injustice and lays down the law to them. There is no hope of conversion; they will die. The poem is interesting from the point of view of the growth of monotheism in Israel, and also from the point of view of the rule of justice in the world (injustice is blamed on the members of the heavenly court; cf. Ps 58). Structure: 1, presentation of God as judge; 2–7, accusation of the unjust judges and sentence; 8, plea of psalmist that the Lord exercise judgment on the earth. **1.** God rises to accuse the elohim beings; cf. 1 Kgs 22:19; Job 1:6ff; Ps 89:6–8; etc. **2–4.** The gods have not fulfilled the charge given them by the Most High to execute justice in favor of the oppressed. **5.** The connection between injustice and the physical world is expressed also in Pss 96:10; 75:3–4; Is 24:1–6; Am 1:2. **7.** The sentence is death—to die like any mortal—a terrible judgment since immortality belonged to the divine sphere. The motif of the fall of the gods (cf. also Ez 28:17; Is 14:15) is borrowed from Canaanite myths. The use made of this text in John 10:34 is conditioned by the contemporary understanding of Jesus' audience. **8.** The appeal is a call to the Lord to activate the condemnation that was just described.

Ps 83. A lament of the community. Despite the nations mentioned in vv 7–9, the specific setting escapes us; the mention of Assyria would point to the 9th–7th centuries. Structure: 2–8, a cry for help against hostile nations; 10–19, God is asked to destroy them, like Israel's enemies in the past. **7–8.** These nine peoples are neighbors, but as a unit they never attacked Israel.

The absence of Babylon could suggest a date before 612 (the fall of Niniveh). **10–12.** The examples are taken from early salvation history: The Kishon river and Endor were scenes of victory (cf. Jgs 4–8). **14–15.** The Lord is asked to destroy them with the east wind, the burning sirocco. **19.** Their defeat will force them to acknowledge the Lord as Elyon, Most High.

Ps 84. A hymn in praise of the Temple, a song of Zion. It is best understood as a song of pilgrims approaching and entering Zion or the Temple (cf. Pss 120–134, the "songs of ascents"). Structure: 2–4, an ardent desire for the Temple; 5–8, the joys of those who make the pilgrimage; 9–10, a prayer for the king; 11–12, the joy and blessings the Temple brings. **2–3.** For this love of the Temple, cf. Pss 42–43; 48:3–4; etc. **4.** The birds nesting, perhaps in the Temple area, become a symbol of the security enjoyed by those who are around "the altars." **6–8.** The text is obscure. Perhaps it is a description of a pilgrimage, where the arid valley becomes a spring, thanks to the early rain. For the theme of water in the desert during the new exodus envisioned by Deutero-Isaiah, see Is 35:6ff; 41:18ff. Then in the Temple the pilgrim *sees* God (softened by the Massoretes to read "appear before"). *through outer and inner wall:* i.e. probably from the city wall to the wall of the Temple. The traditional translation of this phrase has been "from strength to strength"—increasing in strength. **9–10.** The prayer for the king ("anointed") indicates a pre-exilic date; the king is called "shield" (cf. Pss 47:10; 89:19), as protector of the people, and the channel of divine power and blessings. **11.** Cf. Ps 27:4. The comparison of the "wicked" is unexpected, but it can underline the fact that only the faithful, not the wicked, will enjoy God's nearness (as in vv 12–13). **12.** Nowhere else in the Old Testament is God explicitly called "sun," but cf. the association with the sun in Isaiah 60:19–20; Mal 3:29 (4:2).

Ps 85. A lament of the community, to which a divine oracle is given by way of answer. The situation and date cannot be determined, but it is clear that the nation is suffering grievously. Structure: 2–4, see comment below; 5–8, a prayer for restoration to "salvation"; 9–14, an oracle of salvation. **2–4.** These lines have been interpreted of a past event (more probable), such as the restoration from exile, or of a future deliverance (verbs in the prophetic perfect), or against the background of a liturgical re-presentation. **8.** "Salvation," "fidelity" and "kindness" are key terms in this poem; cf. vv 8–14. **9–15.** A prophet (cf. Ps 81:6) speaks and summarizes the divine oracle (v 9) he has received: "shalom," or "peace"—the well-being that is described in the following verses. **11–12.** A bold personification of the Lord's prime qualities and activity; cf. also Is 58:8; 59:14–15.

Ps 86. An individual lament. The psalmist (perhaps the king?) is beset by enemies (14, 17), and looks for a sign from the Lord to confound them. The structure is loose because of numerous borrowings from other psalms: 1–7, a cry for help; 8–10, a hymn of praise; 11–13, request and thanksgiving; 14–17, confident prayers for help. **1.** Cf. Pss 102:3; 40:18. **2.** Cf. Ps 25:20. **3.** Cf. Ps 57:2–3. The use of the term "lord" (Adonai, not *yhwh*) is characteristic of this poem (vv 4–5, 8–9, 12, 15). **8.** The incomparability of Israel's God is an old and frequent theme (Ex 15:11; Ps 77:14; Is 40:18ff), which comes to be understood in a monotheistic sense. **11.** Cf. Ps 25:4–5. Obedience ensures protection by God's "truth" or fidelity to the covenant relation with Israel. **13.** As often elsewhere (e.g. Pss 30:4; 88:4), Sheol is used metaphorically to designate distress, or non-life. **14.** Cf. Ps 54:5. **15.** An old creedal formula is expressed here; cf. Ex 34:6; Ps 103:8; etc. **16.** A maidservant's child is one born in the master's house, and belonging to the master (Ex 34:6); hence the term indicates total devotion.

Ps 87. A hymn of praise, or song of Zion. The text is quite uncertain (see also *NRSV, NJV*). Structure: 1–3, the Lord's choice of Zion as a dwelling; 4–7, Zion as the birthplace of all.

1. The choice of Zion is central to Old Testament belief, and rehearsed many times; cf. Ps 132:13. The threefold repetition of "this one was born here (or, there)" is emphatic, and refers either to Jews of the Diaspora, or to gentiles (cf. v 4) who acknowledge the Lord and so have Zion as their "birthplace." In v 4 God recognizes the two great areas of Fertile Crescent among the worshipers: Babylon and Egypt (called "Rahab" here; cf. Is 30:7). **7.** Singers will cry out, literally, "all my water sources" (roots? home?) are in Zion.

Ps 88. An individual lament, by one who is mortally sick probably (or in great distress)—abandoned by friends and, it would appear, by God. Though unable to understand, the psalmist has the faith and courage to appeal to the Lord. The absence of the motifs of trust and certainty of being heard, so typical of the lament, is conspicuous. Structure: 2–10, a cry for help and the complaint; 10–13, a renewed plea, with the "argument from Sheol" as a motif; 14–19, the final, desperate plea. **4.** The psalmist is in danger of death, on the edge of Sheol, which is described by many images (pit, grave, abyss, etc.). Here the "shades" (11) are "cut off" (6) from the Lord—whence the motif of praising God is used in vv 11–13: there will be no praise offered there (cf. Pss 6:6; 30:9–10). **8.** For the divine "billows," cf. Ps 42:8. **15.** "Hide the face" is a frequent and expressive gesture in the psalms to express divine unconcern or even wrath; see comment on Ps 10:11. It is remarkable that the prayer ends on the grim note of abandonment ("darkness," v 19, also vv 7, 13; cf. Job 10:21–22). M.E. Tate (*Psalms 51–100* [Word Biblical Commentary 20; Dallas: Word, 1990] 404) quotes Martin Marty effectively: "The psalm is a scandal to anyone who isolates it from the biblical canon, a pain to anyone who must hear it apart from more lively words." It deals with a "wintry landscape" of the soul.

Ps 89. A lament of the community, as it stands (vv 39–52!). But it is a mixed composition; the lament is preceded by a hymn in praise of God (2–19) and a rehearsal of the oracle concerning the Davidic dynasty (20–38). The one who prays seems to be identified with a king ("my life," 48; "anointed," 52). The occasion is simply unknown. **2.** The "promises of the Lord" are the actions in history by which the Lord has shown covenant love (Ps 107:43; Is 63:7), in particular the promise to David (vv 3–5). The favors are literally (acts of) *hesed,* a term which, with its correlative of faithfulness (*'emet*), permeates this poem (cf. vv 6, 9, 15, 25, 29, 34, 50). This is a very deliberate move, since these two attributes are not visible at the present time (v 50). **6–8.** For the sons of God who make up the council of the holy ones, see the comment on Ps 82 concerning the heavenly court. **9.** For the incomparability theme, see the comment on Ps 86:8. **10–11.** For the mythological allusions in this version of creation see the comment on Psalm 74:12ff. Like Leviathan, Rahab is a monster personifying the powers of chaos. **15.** See also Ps 97:2. **16.** *the joyful shout:* this particular word is associated with acclamation and procession (of the Ark; 2 Sam 6:15). **19.** For the parallelism of "shield" and "king," see Ps 84:10. **20–38.** An expanded version of 2 Samuel 7; it highlights royal prerogatives that are assured by the Lord: anointing (21), protection (22), victory (23–26), adoptive sonship (27–28), personal and dynastic security (29–38). The promise is unconditional (31–38); individual kings may be punished, but the dynasty will go on (cf. 2 Sam 7:14–16; but see also 1 Kgs 6:12 and Ps 132:12). **39–46.** The complaint begins and is developed in detail; the Lord is accused of having renounced the covenant with David, apparently because of some military disaster. **47–52.** Motifs characteristic of the lament are used to move the Lord to take pity on the king: "how long?"—shortness of life—the contrast between the favors of old and the present insults. **53.** A doxology completes the third book of Psalms (cf. Pss 41:14; 72:18–19).

Ps 90. Probably a community lament, for which no specific occasion can be found. The complaints are general (life is short and troubled), and the poem reflects wisdom influence (v 12). Structure: 1–11, the complaint: God's eternity is contrasted with the fleeting and troubled life of humans; 12–17, a request for God's intervention. **1.** This is the only psalm attributed to Moses; cf. Deut 31:30. **2.** The eternity of God is emphasized to point up the contrast with the brief span of a human being. **3.** The sentence of death is a reversal of the creative act of Genesis 2:7. **4.** The point is the brevity of time for God, exemplified by the sensation of "yesterday" and the night "watch." **5–6.** The MT is obscure, but the theme of the brevity of human life seems to be affirmed; cf. Ps 102:12–13. **7–10.** A description of the sinfulness that arouses the divine wrath. The "biblical" age is three score and ten or, at the outside, 80 years, but these years have little to show. **12.** The prayer is that one may truly appreciate how brief life is and thus obtain wisdom; for the wisdom traits in vv 8–12 cf. Job 4:17–21. **13.** *Have pity on:* literally, "repent concerning," "change your mind about." Moses uses this language (*nhm*) in pleading with God in Exodus 32:12. **15.** The prayer is that the time of affliction be at least equalled by the time of joy. **16.** A spirit of confidence is indicated by the request that future generations will see the divine "glory."

Ps 91. A psalm of trust. Structure: 1–2, an address to one who takes refuge in the Temple; 3–12, the protection that the Lord provides; 14–16, a divine oracle, assuring salvation. **2.** "I say" of the MT is emended to an imperative, "say." One of the Temple personnel advises "trust," and develops the reasons for it: the divine "wings" (Pss 17:8; 36:8; 57:2) and fidelity will give protection from hostile powers (night demons, sun rays, etc.). **8–10.** An affirmation of the traditional view of retribution. **11.** The work of God's angels is illustrated in Genesis 24:7, Exodus 23:20, and Tobit. **12.** The metaphor is derived from the rocky roads in Palestine. **14–16.** This oracle (spoken in the name of the divine "I") confirms the assurance proclaimed in the previous verses.

Ps 92. A song of thanksgiving, preoccupied with retribution for the wicked. Structure: 2–5, introduction in hymnic style, praising the Lord for unspecified "deeds"; 6–9, praise of divine plans, which the wicked fail to understand; 10–16, the Lord rewards the just and punishes the wicked. **5–6.** The reasons for praising God are introduced; the divine works and designs will frustrate the wicked and reward the just. **7–8.** Typical wisdom teaching: the foolish lack understanding and the wicked are destined for punishment ("forever" means an indefinite period). **10.** This verse sounds like an adaptation of the praise of Baal current in Ugarit: "Behold, your enemies, O Baal; Behold, your enemies you shall smite; Behold you will vanquish your foes" (*ANET* 131). **11.** The biblical metaphors of "horn" (="strength" in v 11a) and "rich oil" indicate power and renewal. **12.** It is typical that the downfall of the wicked is witnessed by the just (Pss 37:34; 91:8). **13–15.** For the comparison of the just one to a tree, see Pss 1:3; 37:35; Jer 17:8. **16.** The conclusion underscores the main idea: God's righteous government of the world.

Ps 93. A hymn of praise, commemorating the Lord as king; see comment on Ps 47 about the enthronement psalms. Structure: 1–2, acclamation of the Lord as eternal king and creator; 3–4, divine dominion over the waters of chaos; 5, the divine "decrees" are like the eternal throne (v 2). **1–2.** The cry of enthronement ("The Lord is king") does not preclude kingship from the very beginning (v 2). **3–4.** The waters of chaos, which could just possibly destroy creation, are held in check by divine power; the divine kingship is rooted in creative power. **5.** The "decrees" are the Law. The "holiness" of the Temple is due to the Lord's presence.

Ps 94. A lament, of both an individual and a community. Violence and injustice threaten the community (1–15; cf. Pss

14; 53), and an individual leads the complaint (16–23). There is no need to distinguish two separate psalms. Structure: 1–2. An introductory appeal; 3–7, a complaint about oppression within Israel; 8–15, lessons drawn from wisdom teaching: the Lord will intervene; 16–23, a confident request that justice will be done. **1.** The Lord is a God of vengeance in the sense that it is God who will defend the oppressed and administer justice in the situation described in vv 3–7. **7.** The jeering claim of the wicked is answered by the admonition in vv 8–11 and the encouragement to the upright in vv 12–15. **16–23.** An individual proclaims trust in the Lord's justice (arguing from experience, vv 16–19), probably in the name of the community.

Ps 95. A hymn of praise, commemorating the Lord as king; see comment on Ps 47 about the enthronement psalms. The liturgical character of this hymn, which resembles Psalm 81, is very marked. Structure: 1–5, an exhortation to praise the Lord as king and creator; 6–7a, an exhortation to worship the shepherd of Israel; 7b–11, a prophetic admonition against obstinacy and disobedience. **3.** The exaltation of the Lord beyond all gods is a familiar theme; cf. Ex 15:11 and see the comment on Ps 82. **4–5.** The Lord's kingship stems from creative power. **6–7.** The invitation to enter into the Temple is motivated by the special relationship that the people have to their Shepherd. As in Deuteronomy 30:11–20 and often, "today" indicates a liturgical representation of the ancient bond between God and people. **8.** Probably a prophet is using examples of rebellion in the desert (cf. Ex 17:1–7; Num 20:1–13, for Meribah and Massah; the place names mean "strife" and "testing"). See Heb 3:7–11. **11.** The "rest" meant originally (Deut 12:10; 25:19) the possession of the promised land (which is really the Lord's "rest"); in the context of the psalm it has the overtones of peace with God; the people are reminded where their true rest is (cf. Heb. 4:11).

Ps 96. A hymn of praise, commemorating the Lord as king (see comment on Ps 47). In 1 Chronicles 16:23–33 this song is inserted in the context of David's bringing the Ark to Jerusalem. There is a noticeable similarity to Psalm 98, and many phrases are echoed elsewhere in the Bible (cf. Is 40:9; 42:10). Structure: 1–6, Israel is invited to sing of God's incomparable majesty and creative power; 7–10, an invitation to all nations to worship God as king; 11–13, creation itself is invited to join in the praise of the Lord who comes in judgment. **1.** This is a "new" song perhaps because the liturgical occasion is a new one, or it "re-news" divine praise; cf. Pss 33:3; 40:4; 98:1; Is 42:10. **4–5.** See comment on Ps 95:3; other gods are "zeroes." **6.** These divine attributes are personified as being in attendance upon the Lord; cf. Ps 89:15. **7–9.** Cf. Ps 29:1–2. **10a.** For the cry of enthronement, see comment on Ps 93:1. Some Old Latin and Greek manuscripts added here "from the tree," in reference to the crucifixion of Christ (cf. "regnavit a ligno Deus" of the *Vexilla Regis* hymn). **13.** The coming of the Lord is re-presented in the cult, probably by a procession of the Ark.

Ps 97. A hymn of praise, commemorating the Lord as king (see comment on Ps 47). Structure: 1–5, the cry of enthronement, followed by a description of a theophany; 6–9, universal recognition of the Lord's supremacy and rule; 10–12, assurance of the Lord's care for the faithful. **2–6.** The typical theophanic traits are employed here; cf. Jgs 5:4–5; Deut 33:1–5; Ps 18:8–20. **7–9.** Everyone from the heavens (the "zero" gods over whom God is exalted) to earth (the peoples, and Judah in particular) acknowledges divine rule. For the "most high" (Elyon), see comment on Ps 46:5. **10–12.** A description of the nature of God's rule: care for the righteous.

Ps 98. A hymn of praise, commemorating the Lord as king (see comment on Ps 47). Note the similarity to Psalm 96. Structure: 1–3, an invitation to praise the Lord because of "marvelous deeds"; 4–9, an invitation to all nations and all creation to praise the Lord. There is no obvious historical reference for this psalm. **1–3.** For the "new song," see comment on Ps 96:1. The emphasis here is on the victory or "salvation" which the Lord's arm (cf. Is 51:9; 52:10; 59:16) has wrought. The parallelism between "salvation" and "justice" is typical of Deutero-Isaiah (cf. Is 45:8, 21); so also is the universality (Is 2:1–4; 40:5). **7–9.** See Ps 96:11–13.

Ps 99. A hymn of praise, commemorating the Lord as king (see comment on Ps 47). In contrast to the other enthronement psalms (Pss 47, 93, 95–98), there are no similarities to Deutero-Isaiah, and more emphasis is put on God's relationship to the people. Structure: The refrain of "holy" (vv 3, 5, 9) divides the poem: 1–3, let the nations worship the Lord; 4–5, the divine justice is the reason for worship; 6–8, examples of God's justice in Israel; 9, an exhortation to worship God. **1–3.** A description of the "great" and "high" God invisibly enthroned upon the Ark between the "cherubim," the half-man, half-animal bodyguard (see comment on Ps 80:2). **6–9.** It was through these men that God's justice was dispensed. For the intercession of Moses and Samuel, cf. Jer 15:1. See Exodus 19:9 and 33:9–10 for the "cloud."

Ps 100. A hymn of praise, composed for procession to the Temple. The tone of joy is emphatic and characteristic. An invitation to "all the earth" to praise the Lord blends into a call to Israel to worship God because of the covenant love and fidelity (cf. Ps 117) which demonstrate the divine goodness. **3.** The reason God is to be praised is the covenant relationship with the people. **4.** The exhortation to enter the Temple is probably spoken by the priests; the purpose of the visit is thanksgiving and praise. **5.** How "good" the Lord is, is shown by love (*hesed*) and faithfulness (*'emunah*); see the refrains in Pss 118 and 136.

Ps 101. A royal psalm, spoken by the king, concerning the norms he follows in his rule. Structure: 1–2a, introduction; 2b–8, the royal standards. **1–2.** The justice that he sings of is that which he hopes will characterize his "house" (the royal court). **3–5.** These statements are a kind of negative confession (cf. Pss 15; 24; the conditions for entering the sanctuary); cf. also vv 7–8.

Ps 102. An individual lament, the fifth of the seven penitential psalms. However, the form is unusual in that hymnic (13–18) and prophetic (14, 19–23) elements are incorporated. Structure: 2–12, the appeal and complaint; 13–23, a confident appeal to the Lord as the rebuilder of Zion; 24–25, the personal lament is taken up again; 26–29, conclusion, on the theme of the Lord's eternity. The transition to Zion and restoration has caused great variation in the interpretation of this poem. Is it a natural development (cf. Lam 2:1–17), or the result of the incorporation of another poem? If the entire poem is taken as a unity, the psalmist complains about suffering and then turns confidently to God, more concerned with the fate of the people than with personal destiny. **2–3.** These lines echo many other psalms (cf. Pss 39:13; 27:9; 69:18); on hiding the face, see the comment on Ps 10:11. **4–6.** The suffering seems to proceed from fever and emaciation. "Smoke" is a symbol of the ephemerality of life (Pss 37:20; 68:3). **7–8.** The comparison to the "owl" and the bird alone on a roof underlines the loneliness and desolation. **9.** The fate of the psalmist is wished on people as a "curse." **10.** Mourning and sadness (signified by the ashes) are as much a part of daily existence as eating food. **11.** A "lengthening shadow" portends evening, and here the evening of life, although the psalmist is only in midcourse (v 25). **13.** In contrast to the transitory life of humans (12) is the eternity of God (cf. Ps 90:3–4) which is now proclaimed (and in vv 25–27). God's eternity forms the perspective for the restoration that is desired. **14–18.** The exilic period is the presupposition of this passage, which is filled with confidence and hope. The "glory" (Ez 43:2–4) of the Lord will surely return to Zion. **19–23.** These words are to be written down as a witness for future generations. The restoration will be realized with a conversion of "peoples and kingdoms." **25–27.** There is a return to the contrast between human existence (even, all of creation) and the eternity of God (vv 12–13). Cf. Heb 1:10–12. The metaphor of the clothing in 27 (cf. Is 51:6) underscores the temporary character of creatures. **29.** The final verse comes back to the hope for Israel; something of God's permanence is attached to a future generation of Israelites.

Ps 103. A thanksgiving song of deep religious sensitivity, which could be just as easily termed a song of praise. It is a simple and beautiful reaction to God's goodness. Structure: 1–5, a hymn-like introduction, acknowledging the Lord's goodness; 6–18, the Lord's kindness to the people; 19–22, conclusion. **3.** The parallelism reflects the association of sin and sickness in the Bible (Pss 32:3–5; 107:17; Job, *passim*). **5.** The eagle is a symbol of perennial vigor (Is 40:31). **6–18.** This confession goes from the acts of God in Israel's history to the character of this God whose "kindness" (v 17) has been shown to Israel. **7.** Cf. the prayer of Moses in Ex 33:13. **8.** This is the classical theological formula of Exodus 34:6 (see Num 14:18; Ps 86:15; Jon 4:2). **9.** See Is 57:16. **10.** A noteworthy paradox. **11–18.** The comparisons (cf. Is 55:8–19) come to a climax in the love of a "father" (v 13), which is derived from the intimate knowledge of the people God created—out of dust. **16–18.** The mention of creation leads into a consideration of the brevity of human life, which is contrasted with the enduring love God has for all who keep the covenant. **19–22.** The closing invocation is for the heavenly court and all creation to praise the Lord. The last line forms an *inclusio* with the opening line of v 1.

Ps 104. A hymn of praise of God as creator; one of the most remarkable songs in the psalter. The similarity to the "hymn to the Sun" of Pharaoh Akhenaton (cf. *ANET* 370) has often been noted, esp. for vv 19–23. It would appear that any dependence is largely indirect; the main source of the creation traditions seems to be Genesis 1. Structure: 1–5, an invitation to praise the divine glory in the heavens; 6–18, a description of how God tames watery chaos to serve creation; 19–23, the function of night and day; 24–26, admiration for God's works, especially the sea; 27–30, the dependence of living things upon divine providence; 31–35, conclusion. **1.** The meaning of "bless" the Lord is clear from the parallelism elsewhere with "praise"; one acknowledges the Lord as the source of blessing; see also Ps 103:1. **2–3.** The comparison of "light" to a cloak is easily understood when light is viewed as a "thing" (cf. Job 38:19). God was thought to dwell in a "palace" above the firmament (Gen 1:6–8) and to ride on the clouds (Ps 68:5). **4.** Lightning and winds are merely the divine servants. **5.** The firmness of earth results from a "foundation" (Job 38:4–6). **6–9.** Another description of creation is given in mythological terms: the water of chaos covered the earth, but the Lord brought order out of this with "thunder" (the divine voice), and the waters found their proper place in valleys. The Lord continually watches over creation (v 9). **10–18.** The unruly chaotic waters now have the mission of giving drink to creation and making the earth produce good things for all creatures. A touching scene is evoked by beasts, birds, bread, wine, oil, goats (even the "unessential" rock-badgers, v 18), and humans. **19–23.** A quaint picture: Night is for the beasts and day is for humans to work. The same sequence is found in the Egyptian hymn. The Egyptian sun god retires at night when evil power takes over, but in the psalms, the Lord hears the beasts pray for food. **24–26.** There is a pause to admire the divine wisdom in creation, and especially in the sea. Leviathan is the monster of chaos (Is 27:1), but here a mere plaything (cf. Job 40:25–32). **27–30.** Besides feeding all creatures, God keeps them alive by the creative *ruah* or "breath"; cf. Gen 2:7. God breathes, and creatures live; when God stops breathing, they die (cf. Eccl 12:7). This lively creation poem emphasizes the concept of the world as a continuing event, a continuous creation. **31.** It is characteristic that the author speaks of God's joy in the creation, which reflects the divine glory (Ps 19:2). **35.** The imprecation against sinners does not lessen the power of this poem; it stems from a desire to see a perfect world, in which the divine justice would be manifested. The poem ends with the initial invocation of v 1.

Ps 105. An historical psalm (cf. Pss 78; 106) in hymnic style which ranges from the patriarchs to the conquest (v 44). Structure: 1–6, an invitation to Israel to proclaim God's wondrous deeds; 7–15, the covenant with Abraham and his descendants, and the divine protection; 16–22, the story of Joseph; 23–38, the Exodus from Egypt; 39–43, the marvels in the desert; 44–45, Israel in the land. The first fifteen verses appear in a cultic setting in 1 Chronicles 16:8–22. **1–6.** This introduction calls explicitly for an acknowledgment of the saving events of Israel's history. **7–15.** The covenant with Abraham and the descendants involved the gift of the land (11; v 44). **12–15.** A brief summary of the "wandering" of the ancestors; the term "anointed" for them (15) is not the Genesis tradition. **16–22.** The highlights of the story of Joseph are given; his prediction refers to the interpretation of the dreams in prison. For his "wisdom," cf. Gen 41:29. **23–38.** The sequence of the ten plagues differs from the Exodus account: 9, 1, 2, 4, 3, 7, 8, 10, with no mention of the fifth or sixth plague. **44–45.** The conclusion ties in Sinai (statutes and laws) with the events of sacred history; obedience to the laws is gratitude for salvation.

Ps 106. An historical psalm, conceived in terms of a national lament (unlike Ps 105; cf. Ps 78). Structure: 1–5, the summons to praise God, with a prayer for Israel's prosperity; 6–46, the confession of sin, against the background of the sacred history from Exodus to the period of the Judges; 47, conclusion. In this exilic psalm, history is not used for a recital of praise, but as an expression of sorrow (v 6). The spirit and mood of a lament move through the historical periods as the author emphasizes disobedient and faithless aspects of Israel; praise (implicit) of

God and confession of sin succeed one another. **2.** The mighty deeds of the Lord are incomparable, beyond telling. **4–5.** This prayer asks that the saving deeds of God that are about to be proclaimed be repeated in the present situation (cf. v 47). **6–12.** The confession of sin begins the recital, which follows Exodus 14–15 somewhat freely: rebellion at the Red Sea; deliverance; grateful praise. **13–15.** See Num 11; Ps 78:26–31. **16–18.** Cf. Num 16. **19–23.** See Ex 32. **24–27.** See Num 13–14; Deut 1:19–28; there is a certain exilic coloring to the description (v 27). **28–31.** See Num 25. The rites of Baal of Peor are considered to be made to *dead* gods; only the Lord is a living God. **32–33.** For Meribah, see Ex 17:1–7; Num 20:13; Pss 81:7; 95:8. **34–39.** A picture of continuing infidelity; for human sacrifice, cf. Jer 19:4–5. **40–46.** This seems to reflect the sequence of events that marks the period of the Judges. **47.** A direct reference to Israel in exile; the community begs to be delivered. Verses 47–48 are quoted at the end of a pastiche of psalms in 1 Chronicles 16:35–36. Verse 48 is a doxology, closing the fourth book of Psalms (cf. Ps 89:53).

Ps 107. This poem is characterized by the refrain in 6 and 8, 13 and 15, 19 and 21, 28 and 31, and everything points to a thanksgiving ceremony in the Temple. Structure: 1–3, an invitation to the redeemed to thank God; 4–32, those who were redeemed form four groups: those who made their way out of the desert where they were lost (4–9); prisoners who have been freed (10–16); the sick who have been cured (17–22); sea voyagers who have been rescued (23–32); 33–34, a hymn praising God for the blessings on the (restored) community; these verses lack the double refrain and perhaps are a later addition. If so, the prayer is a post-exilic communal thanksgiving, and the four groups have a symbolic intent (the exiles). **1.** This is a standard summons to praise (1 Chr 16:34; Pss 106:1; 136); the lines may have been recited antiphonally; cf. Ps 118:1–4. **2–3.** There is a clear reference to a community restored from exile (the four corners of the world), although the following groups were not necessarily exiles. The verses may indicate a rereading or reinterpretation of vv 4–32. **4–9.** The desert wanderers were saved by the Lord; the particular incident is unknown. Both this and the "prisoner" theme in 10–16 could easily be applied to the post-exilic community that has come out of exile. **17.** The association between sin and sickness is explicit. **20.** The "word" sent forth by the Lord may refer to an oracle (uttered by a priest?) assuring a cure. **23–32.** A summons to the seafarers who experienced God's "wonders" in the abyss, i.e. the Lord's battle with chaos, the Sea, which was hushed to a mere whisper (29). **33–43.** These verses are reminiscent of Isaiah 35:7; 41:18; 50:2. The punishment of vv 33–34 is reversed for the hungry (vv 35–36). **42–43.** The final verses remind one of Hosea 14:10, a wisdom saying which concludes the work.

Ps 108. A composite psalm, made up of Psalms 57:8–12 (individual lament) and 60:7–14 (lament of the community). Structure: 2–5, a confident hymn which prepares for the request; 6–11, the request and a divine oracle; 12–14, complaint and confident request. Composite psalms which rearrange previous liturgical texts can reflect a new situation, as here. The singer is "among the peoples" (v 4, perhaps in exile?) and calls upon the Lord to appear in a theophany, and to deliver "the loved ones" (6). He is certain of the *hesed* and faithfulness of the Lord (5). The specific request for deliverance (7) is met by a (probably ancient) oracle which lays claim to territory east and west of the Jordan (Shechem and Succoth), maintaining Israel's rights against three traditional enemies (v 10). It is clear from vv 12–14 that the community looks forward confidently to deliverance. **11.** *me:* possibly God if this line is part of the oracle (cf. v 10); more likely this speaker utters a rhetorical question—God will lead Israel. The psalm makes sense in the situation of the exile or some perilous period during the Diaspora. See comment on Pss 57 and 60.

Ps 109. An individual lament. Structure: 1–5, a complaint against the calumny of enemies; 6–19, a series of curses; 20–31, a request that God punish the enemies but bless the psalmist, concluding with a vow of thanksgiving (30–31). The imprecations (vv 6–19) have been interpreted as the words of the psalmist against the enemies. But they can also be interpreted as the charges and curses directed against the psalmist by enemies: the subject is singular, while the enemies are always described in the plural (1–5; 20–31). In v 20 the psalmist wishes the preceding curses to recoil upon the enemies who uttered them. Thus the psalm is an effort to offset the calumny and curses (6–19) that have been directed against the psalmist, perhaps in a legal proceeding. **1–2.** The silence of God contrasts with the words from the deceiving mouths. **6.** An "accuser" (*satan,* the prosecuting attorney, or adversary, the role that is played by "satan" in the Book of Job), is to prosecute the guilty party "at his right hand" (in contrast, God will be at the right hand of the poor, in v 31). The evils envisioned are death and loss of position and possessions, with consequent hardships on the family; even the descendants are to be wiped out, as the curse envelops the whole group (vv 13–15). **16–19.** The specific accusation (v 16) is followed by the application of the talion law to the accused; let his curses clothe and permeate him (vv 17–19). **20.** The psalmist returns the wishes of vv 6–19 upon the accusers and throws himself upon the mercy of God. Instead of persecuting the "poor and needy" (16), he is the one who is "poor and needy" (the Hebrew text repeats the phrase in v 22). **27–28.** The Lord's blessing will offset the enemies' curses and the "hand" of the Lord will be seen in the whole process. **30–31.** The psalmist confidently vows to thank God because the Lord is at the "right hand" of the needy (contrast v 6).

Ps 110. A royal psalm, difficult to understand because of its obscurity (vv 6–7) and textual uncertainty (v 3). It is quoted frequently in the New Testament (vv 1 and 4). Structure: 1–3, an oracle of assurance for the king; 4–7, another oracle concerning royal priesthood and victory. **1.** One of the temple personnel announces an oracle of the Lord to his master, the king. At the Lord's right hand he will vanquish all enemies (cf. v 2). **3.** The text is completely uncertain, and hence obscure. The footnote in the revised *NAB* psalter understands this to be another oracle: divine adoptive sonship of the king is proclaimed. **4.** This oracle is introduced solemnly: the Lord will not "repent" of it, i.e. it is unchangeable. The priestly character of the king is asserted and is associated with Melchizedek, i.e. apparently the dignity of the priest-kings of Jerusalem (cf. Gen 14:18–24). The royal priesthood is "on the model of" Melchizedek's dignity. **5–7.** It is not clear that these words are part of the oracle; they deal with the warring exploits of the king, and v 7 is totally obscure.

Ps 111. A hymn of praise written in acrostic style; the half-lines begin with successive letters of the Hebrew alphabet. The wisdom influence is marked, and many classify this as a wisdom psalm. Indeed it looks as if Psalms 111–112 are a pair, intended to match; if Ps 112 is wisdom, then Ps 111 is the sage's hymn of praise—teaching by example. Cf. v 3 with Ps 112:3, 9; v 4 with Ps 112:4; v 8 with Ps 112:8. Structure: 1, hymnic introduction; 2–9, the reason for praise: the greatness of the works/deeds (the root *'asah* is used six times); 10, a wisdom ending. **1.** Halleluyah is literally "praise Yah," and an *inclusio* with this is formed at the end of v 10. The hymn is intoned in the worshiping community probably by a representative voice, and stress is laid upon inner appreciation ("with all my heart"; cf. Deut 6:4). **2–4.** The events of salvation history are meant; the "renown" of the Lord is indicated in Exodus 34:10; see also Ex 34:6. **5.** The reference is to the manna in the desert (Ex 16; Pss 105:40; 106:14). **6–8.** The grant of Palestine and the Law is commemorated. **9.** Deliverance and covenant are in parallelism. **10.** A wisdom tag line; cf. Prov 1:7; 9:10. In this psalm salvation history is being inculcated by wisdom teachers.

Ps 112. Like Psalm 111, this is written in acrostic style, portraying the ideal wise person. See also Ps 1. There is no particular structure, but merely typical wisdom sayings (cf. Ps 37). **1.** Cf. Ps 1:2. **3.** See v 9b and Ps 111:3. **8.** The just person will eventually witness the downfall of enemies; cf. Pss 54:9; 118:7. Similarly, the wicked will witness the exaltation of the just (vv 9–10); cf. Prov 10:28.

Ps 113. A hymn of praise. Structure: 1–3, summons to praise; 4–6, exaltation of the Lord; 7–9, proclamation of God's care for the poor. **1.** Halleluyah continues as a superscription, and Psalms 113–118 are called the Egyptian Hallel, as opposed to the simple Hallel, Psalms 146–150. The great Hallel designates Psalms 120–136 (songs of ascents), or Psalms 135–136, or just Psalm 136. "Servants of the Lord" are perhaps priests and Levites, but it could refer to all the faithful. **7–9.** These lines follow from the lofty position (vv 6–7) of the Lord who can easily see and deliver the lowly and unfortunate; cf. Ps 35:10 and 1 Sam 2:1–10 (song of Hannah). God's majesty is manifested also in mercy. The Halleluyah which ends this psalm may belong to the next one, as in Psalms 111–113.

Ps 114. A hymn of praise (joined to Psalm 115 in LXX and Vulgate). The usual hymnic introduction is lacking. The poem recalls vividly the saving deeds of the Exodus and conquest; the association of the two crossings, Red Sea and Jordan, appears already in Joshua 4:23–24. **1–2.** There is a rapid move from Exodus to the period of the monarchy, with the separation of Judah and Israel. **3.** The reaction of the sea is due to the theophany of v 7. Sea is personified; it flees without fighting (the background is that of the myth of the battle between a god and the sea; cf. *ANET* 130–131; Hab 3:8; Pss 77:17; 104:7). **4.** The mountains are probably those of Sinai, trembling at the theophany (v 7). **5–6.** The dramatic repetition of the questions in these verses sets up the climactic ending (7–8; cf. Ex 17:6; Num 20:11).

Ps 115. A choir song of Temple liturgy, perhaps a lament; certainly distinct from Psalm 114, with which it has been connected in some Hebrew mss. and ancient versions. Structure: 1–3, a motif from a lament; 4–8, a hymnic satire about idols; 9–18, a liturgical dialogue. **1–3.** An implicit request, that will be realized by the Lord alone, who acts for the sake of the "Name" (cf. Ez 20), not by Israel. The ridicule of the "nations" is dramatized in v 2 (cf. Pss 42:4, 11; 79:10) and is answered by a confident statement about "our God" in v 3, and in the ensuing description of the ineffectiveness of idols. **4–8.** A satire against dead idols in the style of Jer 10:3–16; Is 40:18–20; 44:9–20; Wis 13:10–15:17. As Israel deepened its idea of monotheism, any image was seen as representing zero; hence eyes, but no vision, etc. Notice the imprecation in v 8. **9–11.** The mention of Israel, Aaron and God-fearers (congregation, priests and perhaps proselytes) occurs again in vv 12–13 and in Ps 118:1–4. The refrain in 9–11 may be an antiphonal response. **12–13.** These lines seem clearly to be a response ("us"). **14–18.** Verses 14–15 are a blessing uttered by a solo (priestly?) voice, while vv 16–18 represent the response of the community. The blessings of the Lord have to do with life—the very opposite for those who are dead in the "silence" of Sheol; they cannot praise the Lord (v 17; cf. Pss 88:11–13; 94:17); to live is to praise God.

Ps 116. A thanksgiving hymn, divided (after v 9) into two psalms in the LXX and Vulgate. The life setting is probably the Temple (19) where one who has been delivered from dire distress (Death and Sheol, v 3) fulfills vows (vv 14, 18) with a "sacrifice of thanksgiving" (17). Structure: 1–2, acknowledgment of the Lord's response to prayer; 3–4, description of past distress; 5–9, a lesson (for bystanders) is to be seen in the way the Lord saved the psalmist; 10–11, a flashback (cf. Ps 30:7–

11); 12–19, acknowledgment of the Lord as rescuer. **3.** See the comment on Ps 18:5 for the imagery here. **4.** To "invoke the name of the Lord" here means to ask for help, but in vv 13, 17 it means to proclaim the sacred name in thanksgiving. **5–6.** The didactic tendency of the thanksgiving psalm is exemplified here: a lesson is preached to those who are present. **13.** The "cup of salvation" seems to be part of a libation rite. **15.** The death of the Lord's faithful (such as the psalmist had been faced with) is "precious" in the Lord's eyes—this seems to mean that the Lord will not let his faithful ones (such as the psalmist) die. For the blood (=death) being "precious," see Ps 71:14b; the faithful are too precious to be allowed to die. **16.** For the "child of your maidservant," see comment on Ps 86:16.

Ps 117. A hymn of praise, the shortest psalm in the psalter. The structure is a model of hymn style: the summons to praise, followed by the reason for it. The gentiles are invited to praise the Lord because of the saving acts performed in favor of Israel: these are the acts of *hesed* and *'emet,* love and fidelity, which are the enduring qualities of God's relationship with Israel.

Ps 118. A thanksgiving liturgy. This psalm has received many varying interpretations. As a whole it is a thanksgiving liturgy. Structure: 1–4, a summons to praise (Israel, Aaron, God-fearers); 5–18, a thanksgiving song of an individual, that has affinity to the gate liturgies (Pss 15; 24); a victory song is contained in 15–16; 19–29, a proclamation and liturgical procession. It is tempting to understand the "I" as the king, who heads a public thanksgiving and procession to the Temple. Jewish tradition associated the poem with the joyous feast of Tabernacles. **1–4.** The whole community is addressed in v 1, and then a summons is issued to each of three groups (also mentioned in that order in Ps 115:9–11; cf. Pss 106:1; 107:1; 135:19–20). **5.** If the "I" is not the king, he is not the one who addressed the groups in vv 1–4. A thanksgiving psalm begins here, expressing great trust in the Lord (6–9); note the sapiential style: (it is) "better to . . ." **10.** The nations are not identified; there are echoes of the royal psalms (Ps 18:29–30, 36–39). **14.** The language recalls Exodus 15:2. **15–16.** The "right hand" is God's instrument of victory; cf. Ex 15:6, 12. **17.** Physical death is meant, and a full life on earth is implied. **18.** The Lord's punishment is seen as a chastisement in the sense of Proverbs 3:11–12. **19–20.** The gates of justice are the gates of the Temple, where the justice of the one who enters is emphasized (Pss 15; 24), and through which only the just, i.e. the "victors," shall enter. **22.** The symbol of the cornerstone is derived from the practice of stonemasons to choose only the best to be in a key position of the building. Here it stands for the psalmist whose stressful experience and restoration has been described. The New Testament interpretation (Mt 21:42; Acts 4:11; etc.) sees a more eminent fulfillment in Christ. The verse could be proclaimed by the community that speaks (vv 23–24). The "day the Lord has made" is the day the Lord acted and saved (v 16). **25.** "Hosanna" is a shortened form of the Hebrew *hosiʿa-nnaʾ*, "save us." **26–27.** These lines are suitable for an entrance liturgy; for v 27 see Num 6:25. In 27b a command is given to the community to execute a procession to the horns of the altar. **29.** An inclusion with v 1.

Ps 119. An acrostic poem of 176 verses. Each of the eight verses of the first strophe begins with the first letter of the Hebrew alphabet (*aleph*); each verse of the second strophe begins with the second letter (*beth*); and so on for all 22 letters of the alphabet. There are eight verses to a strophe, and in practically every verse a synonym for the Torah or teaching is to be found: decrees, ways, precepts, statutes, commands, ordinances, words, instruction. Thus the entire work is in praise of the Law, and of the joys to be found in observance. It is not legalism, but a love and desire for the word of God that communicated the divine will to the people. There is no logical progression of thought, nor is there any simple classification, since there are found here echoes of hymns, laments, and wisdom. **2.** For wholehearted devotion, inspired by Deuteronomy 6:4, see vv 10, 34, 58, 69, 145. **14.** The note of joy in the observance of Law is mentioned frequently: vv 24, 35, 47, 70, 77, 92, 111, 174; the comparison with riches is characteristic of the doctrine of the sages. **19.** The Hebrew *ger* (sojourner or wayfarer) is one who has no claim to possession of territory; the meaning is spiritualized here to indicate one for whom the Lord alone is the only claim; the pilgrim seeks not land, but to know the Lord's will. **22–23.** Motifs from the individual lament appear often, as here, and in vv 28, 49–54, 61, 81–88, 132–136, 153–158. **25.** Note the connection between word and life; cf. vv 28, 107. **34.** "Understanding" is meant in a religious sense, like "fear of the Lord"; cf. vv 73, 135, 144. **83.** Containers for wine or water were often made of leather, and would become brittle in the warmth of a home. **89.** See Is 40:8; Ps 89:3. **96.** The thought is obscure. Perhaps he recognizes that fulfillment of God's "commandment" (described as exceedingly broad) falls short of what it should be. **120.** Strong language for fear or awe before the Lord. **147–148.** Through the night the psalmist awaits the divine message. **150–151.** Note the contrast between far and near. **159.** See v 40. **162.** The metaphor of rich spoil is to suggest only the rejoicing of the psalmist.

Ps 120. The precise interpretation of "Songs of Ascents" (Pss 120–134) is hard to determine. They have been called also "gradual psalms" (from the Latin *gradus,* or step), as though they had been sung on various steps in the Temple. They are generally understood to be a collection of pilgrimage songs for those who would "ascend" to the Jerusalem Temple. This psalm is an individual lament by one who is beset by enemies in a hostile area. Structure: 1–2, a confident appeal; 3–4, an imprecation; 5–7, a complaint about the present situation. **1.** The psalmist's past experience is the reason for the appeal in v 2. **3–4.** These verses are directed against the enemy. Verse 3 derives from the common self-imprecation formula, "Thus may the Lord do so, and more" (cf. 2 Sam 3:9). **4.** The broom plant burns with intense heat. **5–7.** Meshech is the name of an ancient people of northeast Asia Minor. Kedar is the name of a desert tribe from north Arabia. These two places are so far apart that it is likely that they are metaphorical for "barbarians."

Ps 121. A psalm of trust, characterized by the repetition (6 times) of the term "guard." Structure: 1–2, question and answer; 3–8, an address to the psalmist. **1.** The "mountains" probably refer to the Jerusalem Temple. **2.** The question as to the source of the help is answered: the Lord. **3–8.** A strong affirmation of the Lord's "guarding" of the psalmist and of Israel, probably uttered by one of the Temple personnel; cf. Ps 91:3–13. **5–6.** The possibility of sunstroke in Palestine is real (cf. Is 49:10), and many superstitions about the effect of the moon (cf. Ps 91:5–6) exist.

Ps 122. A song of Zion, on the occasion of a pilgrimage to Jerusalem. Structure: 1–2, arrival at Jerusalem, the cause of joy; 3–5, praise of Zion; 6–9, prayers for Jerusalem. **1–3.** On arrival, the pilgrim recalls the joy with which the invitation to make the pilgrimage was received. **3–5.** A proclamation of the religious significance of the holy city, the place of worship since David had transferred the Ark there (Ps 132), and there also was the place of "judgment" (1 Kgs 7:7). **6–9.** The prayers for Jerusalem are centered upon "peace" or *shalom,* which can be seen as reflected in the name, Jerusalem; *nomen est omen.*

Ps 123. A confident plea, reflecting an exilic or post-exilic attitude. **1–2.** A representative of the community speaks (v 1, "I" and "our"). **2.** The comparison with the alert "eyes" of servants is especially fine; as one looks to the largesse (as well as the command) that comes from the "hands" of the master, so Israel looks expectantly to the Lord. **3–4.** The "contempt" which has occasioned the prayer cannot be further specified.

Ps 124. A thanksgiving song of the community. Structure: 1–5, a description of a threat from an unnamed "people"; 6–8, thanksgiving for deliverance. **1–5.** A vivid repetitious expression of what would have been, without the Lord's help. The metaphors echo the myth of the unruly waters (chaos; Jon 2:4; Ps 69:2–3). **6–7.** The metaphors change to those of the teeth of a wild animal, and a fowler's trap (a wooden instrument, with nets triggered to capture the prey). **8.** Cf. Pss 121:2; 146:5–6.

Ps 125. A national psalm of trust. Structure: 1–2, an affirmation of trust, which dominates the psalm; 3–5, a prayer for the upright. **1–2.** The reasons for trust are the inviolability of Zion (cf. Ps 46:6), and the protection of the Lord who "surrounds" the people just as the mountains "surround" Jerusalem. **3.** The basis for hope is that for the sake of the just, wickedness *must* disappear from the land. The metaphor of the "scepter" refers to either internal or external oppression. **4–5.** An appeal for the Lord's just judgment upon the good and the wicked. The poem, like Ps 128:6, concludes with a prayer for Israel's prosperity (cf. also Ps 122:8).

Ps 126. A lament of the community. Structure: 1–3, an historical survey; 4–6, a prayer for restoration. **1–3.** The reference is to the end of the exile. The return could hardly be believed (like a dream) at first. Some interpreters refer these verses to a future deliverance. **4.** The implication is that the return from exile was not all that it had been envisioned to be. In the poet's own time, the Lord's continuing intervention is needed. The comparison to the wadies in the Negeb bears on the transformation undergone by the dry, caked valley, once water courses through it. **5.** This has the air of a proverb which is explained more fully in v 6. The toil and labor involved in planting will be followed by the joy of the harvest.

Ps 127. A wisdom psalm (note the ascription to Solomon, who was reputed for wisdom and for building). The structure of this psalm pivots on the theme of building: a house (1–2), a family (3–5). **1.** A very vivid comparison, and for the theme of guarding, see Ps 121. **2.** The Lord is the giver of every gift, no matter the human effort; this is expressed paradoxically in the contrast between hard work and "sleep"—God gives as God pleases. **4–5.** The comparison of sons to arrows lies in the protection that they provide for a family, as specified in v 5; in the judicial processes that take place at the "gate" of the city, the many sons will support the father.

Ps 128. Like Psalm 127, a wisdom psalm. Ps 128:2–3 resembles Ps 127:3–5; the common theme is children. Structure: 1–4, a beatitude formula which is spelled out for the family (note the inclusion of 1 and 4); 5–6, a blessing on the individual and on Zion. **1.** Fear of the Lord is interpreted as walking in God's ways. **2–4.** The reward for such fear of God is prosperity and a large progeny. **5–6.** These lines present a blessing from the Lord (pronounced by a priest? cf. Ps 134:3) that points to the basis of Jewish happiness: the good of Jerusalem. The final line repeats Ps 125:5.

Ps 129. The genre is difficult to determine; perhaps a lament of the community. Structure: 1–4, a summary of Israel's sad history of oppression/deliverance (from Exodus to Exile?); 5–8, a prayer that Israel's enemies be punished. Some interpreters regard vv 1–4 as a thanksgiving of the community (cf. Ps 124). **1–2.** The history of Israel's oppression is compared to that of one who has barely survived. "Let Israel say" may indicate a liturgical recital by an individual who speaks for the community. **3–4.** Israel was not merely used as a beast of burden, but she was herself plowed up, until the Lord broke the cords that enslaved her. **6–7.** The grass that happens to grow on the roofs of beaten earth has no root and cannot last, and cannot be harvested. **8.** Blessing, such as that of the harvesters (Ru 2:4), will be absent from the enemies (who have been compared to unharvested grass in vv 5–6).

Ps 130. An individual lament, popularly known by its Latin incipit, "De profundis"; one of the seven penitential psalms. Structure: 1–2, a cry for forgiveness; 3–6, reasons for trust; 7–

8, an exhortation to the community. **1.** The "depths" are the watery deep, chaos, the sphere of death and Sheol, far from God. **3.** This poignant question underlines the generosity of forgiveness that is God's gift to those who fear him ("that you may be revered"; cf. 1 Kgs 8:39–40). **5–7.** The "word" so ardently awaited by the psalmist may be an oracle of salvation from the priest, indicating the divine forgiveness. If so, then Israel is urged to learn from this experience: the Lord does forgive (v 8). Verse 7a is repeated in Ps 131:3a.

Ps 131. A psalm of trust. The writer offers loyalty and modest achievement to God, grateful for the security and satisfaction that God provides. Structure: 1, a statement of personal humility and limitations; 2, an affirmation of childlike trust; 3, a recommendation to Israel. **2.** This tender comparison to a "weaned child" indicates the trusting reliance upon the Lord. **3a.** See Ps 130:7a; perhaps it is a liturgical adaptation of the prayer.

Ps 132. A royal psalm, concerning the oath of David (1–10) and the oath of the Lord (11–18). David swore to provide a dwelling for the Lord; the Lord's oath is the choice of Zion and the line of David. The liturgical setting can only be guessed at: New Year, or perhaps a covenant festival. Structure: 1–5, a prayer for David for his concern (interpreted as an "oath") about the Lord's tabernacle; 6–10, a description of the procession of the Ark; 11–13, the Lord's promise of an eternal dynasty; 14–18, the Lord's eternal choice of Zion. **1–5.** This is an imaginative and expanded version of 2 Sam 6–7. The lines are presumably spoken by a priest or cultic official. **6.** *We have heard of it in Ephrathah:* This seems to be a vivid re-creation of the discovery of the Ark ("it") in the fields of Jaar, i.e. Kiriath-jearim (see 1 Sam 7:1–2). The exhortation in v 7 suggests the role of a choir or community leader. **8.** This is a liturgical cry; cf. Num 10:35; 2 Chr 6:41–42. The Lord advances, enthroned on the Ark ("footstool"), borne by priests in a lively procession.

11. The dynastic oracle is described as an oath (cf. Ps 89:4): the dynasty will be eternal, *provided* (contrast Ps 89:20–38, where the covenant with David is unconditional) the descendants are faithful to the covenant and decrees (v 12). **14–18.** A description of the blessings that flow from the Lord's choice of Zion. **16.** Cf. v 9. The "horn" (v 17) is David's strength, his descendants, and so also, in parallelism, is the "lamp."

Ps 133. The genre of the poem is hard to determine but it is ideally suited as one of the pilgrim psalms; it praises unity, without specifying within a family or a larger group. The emphasis is on the place where the group is: Zion. Where the people are at one is Zion, for there (v 3) the Lord has given his blessing. Structure: 1, an expression of admiration of the unity of Israel; 2–3, two comparisons for the blessings that descend upon them there in Zion. **2.** The oil has been poured out generously and runs down the beard; the allusion seems to be to the anointing of the high priest. The oil itself is a symbol of refreshment. **3.** Mount Hermon is a majestic peak in the Anti-Lebanon range, and presumably it provided refreshment, water and dew, for those nearby. But it is surpassed by the dew of Zion, where the Lord has pronounced blessing: "life forever," i.e. full and overflowing.

Ps 134. A liturgical blessing, which is the last of the songs of ascents. Structure: 1. The "servants of the Lord" (probably priests or a choir) are exhorted to praise the Lord, perhaps in an evening ceremony. 2–3. The blessing of the Lord by the people will be matched by the divine blessing of Zion. Verse 3 underlines the importance of Zion as a channel of divine blessing (cf. also Ps 124:8), and it is perhaps directed to a pilgrim ("you" is in the singular).

Ps 135. A hymn of praise echoing in part Psalm 115. The life setting is the Temple (vv 1–2). Structure: 1–4, introduction; 5–18, a speaker proclaims reasons for praise: God's supremacy in creation and in salvation history and also the futility of idolatry (15–18; cf. v 5); 19–21, conclusion. Many of the verses are repeated from other parts of the Bible in the style of the so-called anthological composition. **1.** "Servants" of the Lord are normally the priests (cf. Ps 134:1), but the term is also applicable to the community (cf. v 19a). **5.** A solo voice is indicated. On the divine supremacy over "other gods," see the comment on Ps 82 and cf. Ex 15:11. **6.** Cf. Ps 115:3. More detailed reasons for praise now follow: God's creative activity, the "signs and portents" in the redemption and settlement of the people. **13–18.** This is virtually identical with Psalm 115:4–8; see comment there. **19–21.** The community, the priests, Levites and God-fearers are invited to bless the Lord; cf. Ps 115:9–11.

Ps 136. A hymn of praise in the form of a litany; often called the Great Hallel. Structure (cf. Ps 135): 1–3, introduction; 4–22, praise because of the Lord's creative power and saving actions on behalf of Israel (cf. Ps 135:6–12); 23–26, conclusion. The song can be designed for antiphonal rendering: the first line by a soloist, and the refrain by the congregation. **4–9.** The cosmological picture is much the same as that of Genesis 1; as in the Pentateuch, creation serves as a prelude to the salvation history. **13–15.** Unlike Psalm 135, the events of the Red Sea are commemorated. **17–22.** These events are almost the same (without refrain) as Ps 135:10–12. **23–25.** The conclusion embraces the present community ("us") in the gracious interventions of God. **26.** The final verse forms an inclusion with v 1, as often in the hymns.

Ps 137. A lament of the community which dates from the Exile or post-exilic period. Structure: 1–3, a flashback to earlier experiences in the Exile; 4–6, an imprecation on one who would forget Jerusalem (the poet); 7–9, an imprecation on those who destroyed Jerusalem. **1.** The reference is to the settlement of the exiles in Babylon, where countless irrigation canals from the Tigris and Euphrates watered the plain. **3.** The request of the captors is analogous to the frequent question motif which appears in the lament, "Where is your God" (e.g. Ps 79:10). The "songs of Zion" has been adopted as a classification of certain hymns (Pss 46, 48, 76, 84, 87, 122). **4.** The question implies that the "foreign" land is unclean as well as hostile. **5–6.** While delivering this imprecation, the psalmist is at the same time singing a song of Zion! The reference to hand and tongue is in view of harp and song. It is not clear what happens to the right hand (MT has "forget"; others read the verb as "wither"). **7.** Edom ravaged Judah with the fall of Jerusalem (Lam 4:21; Ob 8:15). **9.** All warfare is barbaric and no one practice is more brutal than another. Ancient and modern warfare involve atrocities (cf. Hos 10:14; 14:1; Nah 3:10); the mention of children here is a cliché that sums up the usual horrors of war. The point is that the writer is asking for the implementation of the talion law: let Babylon be punished in payment for what she did to the Israelites. The talion law (Ex 21:23–25; Lev 24:17–22; etc.) was designed to produce equity in punishment.

Ps 138. A thanksgiving psalm. Structure: 1–3, thanksgiving for deliverance; 4–6, hymn-like proclamation of the universal recognition of God; 7–8, expression of trust and acknowledgment of the Lord's work. **1.** Hebrew *'elohim* can stand for God, "gods," and angels (the members of the heavenly court); cf. Ex 15:11; Pss 82; 86:8. **2.** That this prayer is uttered in the court of the Temple is suggested by v 2a. **3.** A summary statement of the Lord's saving intervention. **4–5.** This idealistic and enthusiastic universalism is characteristic also of other psalms (Pss 22:28–30; 66:1–4; and the enthronement psalms). **6.** The Lord's very height provides a view of everything; cf. Ps 113:5–6. **8.** The poet returns to the notion of the Lord's *hesed,* or love (cf. v 2), that is the reason for the trust and confidence expressed in v 7.

Ps 139. The classification is uncertain: a hymn, or a sapiential consideration of God's active presence, or the prayer of an accused person (vv 19–24). It is possible that this is really an affirmation of innocence—this would be the thrust of vv 19–

24—that is preceded by considerations concerning God's loving presence. The "I-Thou" character of this poem makes it one of the most personal and beautiful expressions in the Bible. Structure: 1–6, praise of God because of intimate knowledge of the psalmist; 7–12, the impossibility of escaping from the Lord's presence; 13–19, praise of God for the divine involvement in the very birth and predestination of the speaker; 19–24, a plea to see divine justice at work, and to remain faithful. **1.** Full of trust and admiration, the psalmist approaches the Lord, the omniscient God who "probes" and "knows" a loyal follower (cf. vv 23–24). **2.** Sitting and standing is Semitic idiom for completeness, hence "at all times." **7.** In an imaginative flight, the poet describes how one cannot escape the Lord's presence or "spirit." Were one to be taken like Elijah (2 Kgs 2:9–10), or to sink to the depths of Sheol like Korah and Dothan (Num 16:29–33), there is no escape. Although there is no loving contact with God in Sheol, this does not mean that it is beyond divine reach (cf. Am 9:2). **9–10.** The speed with which the dawn comes will not suffice to evade the "hand" of God, no matter where the poet might flee. **13–15.** The mystery of gestation is open to God—another sign of intimate presence to the poet. By "depths of the earth" is meant the womb, but the phrase may originally have reflected the story of the creation of humans from "mother" earth (Gen 2:7). **16.** God is thought to have the names of all inscribed in a book (cf. Pss 56:9; 69:29). **17–18.** An expressive indication of divine transcendence; on God's thoughts, see Is 55:8. **19–20.** There is an abrupt transition to this personal problem. The psalmist is opposed to the wicked who are considered personal foes, and wants to see the divine justice at work. **21–22.** Somewhat glibly, personal enemies are identified as the enemies of God as well. As such they are seen as hateful ("hatred" is not primarily emotional). This amounts to a declaration of loyalty: as if to say, "your enemies are my enemies." As sinners, the enemies of God are worthy of rejection, but it should be added that it is for God to determine who these are, not the psalmist. **23–24.** These verses soften considerably the apparently self-righteous tone of the preceding lines. There is no complacency here ("probe me"), but rather a recognition of the possibility that the *way* of the psalmist is crooked. Should there be any wavering in personal loyalty, that same God who knows all things is also able and willing to bring about a change and lead into the *paths* of old.

Ps 140. An individual lament. The poet is beset by calumnies of the wicked, but the description is too general to permit of specific conclusions (cf. Ps 64). Structure: 2–4, a cry for help against the enemies; 5–8, a plea, complaint, and expression of trust; 9–12, a plea for God's judgment on the wicked; 13–14, certainty that the prayer has been heard. **4.** For similar metaphors, cf. Pss 52:4; 58:5; 64:4. **5–6.** For the metaphor of the trap, cf. Pss 9:16; 64:6; and comment on Ps 124:7. **10–12.** Although the text is somewhat uncertain, the poet invokes the talion law (see comment on Ps 137:9), and wishes to see the enemies defeated by their own devices; cf. comment on Ps 7:15.

Ps 141. An individual lament. Structure: 1–2, a cry for help; 3–7, a prayer not to be led astray by the wicked who will certainly be judged; 8–10, a confident plea. **2.** In the liturgy God accepts sacrifice—so also may the prayer of the psalmist be received, like "incense." **4–5.** The real fear is to be seduced by the wicked (cf. Ps 84:11); hence any discipline from the righteous can only be beneficial. **6–7.** The MT is uncertain and obscure; the sequence of ideas seems to call for the punishment and judgment of the wicked. **10.** The "nets" are those that the wicked prepared for the just (cf. Ps 140:6, 12).

Ps 142. An individual lament, which is characterized by simplicity, humility, and trust. Structure: 2–4, an appeal to God; 4–5, the complaint; 6–8, a confident request and a vow to give thanks. **1–3.** The only recourse is to the mercy of God. **5–6.** With no one to help, the psalmist must rely upon the Lord as "refuge" (a term that occurs more often in the psalter than elsewhere) and as "portion" (a spiritualization of the term originally used of the apportionment of the land; cf. Num 18:20). **8.** One should not press too hard on "prison" which could be merely a metaphor for a deathly condition; cf. Lam 3:6–9. The purpose of the deliverance is, as so often, the opportunity to praise God along with the community of the "just."

Ps 143. An individual lament; the seventh penitential psalm, which echoes the phraseology of other psalms. Structure: the repetitious character of the lines renders any division rather arbitrary; the first half seems more desperate than the verses that follow. **1–2.** The appeal is to God's fidelity and grace; the psalmist admits sinfulness, and appeals to the divine mercy. The "justice" (v 1) is God's ability and will to save. **3.** See Ps 7:6. Darkness is associated with the abode of the dead; cf. Job 10:21–22. **5–6.** The thought of the saving acts in the days of old is a consolation, and a reason to plead with God; cf. Ps 77:12–13. **7.** For the hiding of the divine face, see the comment on Ps 10:11. The "pit" is, of course, Sheol (cf. Pss 28:1; 30:4; etc.). **8.** As often in the psalms, dawn is the time when God answers (cf. Ps 5:4). **10–12.** This plea is typical of the sincerity that characterizes this prayer: "you are my God"—"I am your servant." See also Ps 51:12–14 for the action of the divine spirit.

Ps 144. The classification is difficult. The poem is an echo of other psalms, especially Ps 18, and it has elements of both the lament and thanksgiving. It may even be called a royal psalm (cf. v 10). Structure: 1–2, thanksgiving for divine aid; 3–4, the motif of human frailty; 5–8, plea for deliverance; 9–11, vow of thanksgiving and refrain (cf. vv 7b, 8); 12–15, communal prayer for prosperity. **1–2.** Cf. Ps 18:2, 35, 47. **3.** Cf. Ps 8:5. **4.** On this theme, cf. Pss 39:6; 102:12; Job 7:16; 8:9. **5–7.** Cf. Ps 18:10–17. As so frequently in the Bible, the mighty waters symbolize the powers of chaos and death. **12–14.** The text is obscure, and its connection with the previous lines is difficult to ascertain. The blessings of food and children, and of safety, seem to be associated with the king through whom God communicates divine blessing. **15.** Cf. Ps 33:12.

Ps 145. A hymn of praise in acrostic pattern (cf. Ps 111; each verse begins with successive letters of the alphabet: *aleph, beth,* etc.). Structure: 1–3, hymnic introduction (by an individual, throughout); 4–9, Israel's praise of the divine deeds and words; 10–20, God's own works proclaim that the Lord (10, 14, 17, 18) is king, provider and savior; 21, conclusion. **3.** Cf. 96:4. **5–8.** Cf. Ps 111:2–4; the reference here is to creation and salvation history; for v 8, cf. Ex 34:6. **15–16.** The beneficent providence of God reflected in these lines has made them a popular prayer, especially at mealtime, in the Christian tradition. See also Ps 104:27–28.

Ps 146. A hymn of praise. The psalter ends with five Halleluyah psalms (Pss 146–150; i.e., they begin and end with the exclamation, "praise Yah"); see comment on Ps 113:1. Structure: 1–2, hymnic introduction; 3–4, admonition on the vanity of trusting in mortals; 5–10, hymnic development of the Lord as creator and savior—the reasons for relying upon God (v 5). **1–2.** Cf. Ps 104:1, 33. **3–4.** The frequent motif of human mortality (cf. Ps 90:2–3) is used to point up the contrast to the following verses in which the Lord is praised as one to be trusted in every crisis. The "princes" are a symbol for powerful and rich leaders. **5–10.** This catalogue of divine attributes is typically concrete and describes the way Israel conceived of the Lord. **7.** These actions recall the Exodus events. **9.** Strangers, widows and orphans were the unfortunate, protected by law (Ex 22:20–21), but often neglected.

Ps 147. This hymn of praise can be divided into three parts, each introduced by an invitation to sound the praises of God: 1–6, praise of the Lord as restorer of Israel and creator; 7–11, God's providential direction of nature; 12–20, God's care for Zion and Israel and the divine control of nature. This poem reflects many psalms (Pss 33, 104; and see Is 40). **2.** The reference is to the end of the exile. **3.** Cf. Is 61:1. **4.** Cf. Is 40:26–28. **5.** Surprisingly, references to the Lord's wisdom are relatively late in the Old Testament. **8–9.** This is *creatio continua.* **10–11.** Material advantages are of little account (cf. Ps 33:16–17; Prov 21:31); one must fear the Lord. **13–14.** These are the primary blessings that Israel hoped for; cf. Pss 127–128. **15–18.** The "word" of God is responsible for the cycle of the seasons described in these verses. **19–20.** A special divine word is reserved to Israel; cf. Deut 4:8; 32:8–9.

Ps 148. A hymn that is really a summons to praise, addressed to all in the heavens (1–6, with the reason in 5b–6) and to all on earth (7–12, with the reason in 13–14). It is reminiscent of the "Benedicite" canticle, or Song of the Three Children (Dan 3:52–90, Greek text). **4.** On "highest heavens," see the note in the revised *NAB*. **5b.** Cf. Ps 33:9. **7.** In contrast to v 4, the chaotic depths are mentioned here. **13.** For the symbol of horn (=strength), see Pss 132:17; 112:9.

Ps 149. A hymn of praise. Structure: 1–4, an invitation to the community to praise the Lord because of what has been done for them; 5–9, an exhortation describing the warlike mood of the participants as they prepare to carry out the divine judgments. It is not possible to associate this song with a specified historical event. **1.** For the "new" song, see comment on Ps 96:1. **6–7.** Some kind of victory ritual seems to be reflected in these lines. **9.** For an interpretation of the "glory of all God's faithful," see the note in the revised *NAB*.

Ps 150. Book Five of the psalter closes with this doxology (see Ps 105:48): a hymn of praise which is almost entirely a hymnic introduction ("praise" occurs 11 times, besides the opening and closing halleluyah). The poem answers the questions, where (1), why (2) and how (3–5). **1.** The heavenly sanctuary is meant. The members of the heavenly court are called to join the universal chorus of praise; cf. Ps 29. **6.** This verse matches v 1; now all on earth combine to give praise.

General Index to Part I